"Jennifer Cork's *What's Your Anxiety Level?* is a game-changing resource for neurodivergent kids and teens with anxiety. As an autistic individual, I know how valuable this would have been. Rooted in affirming, research-backed CBT adaptations, it empowers kids with self-regulation tools while respecting their needs – a must-read for clinicians and caregivers!"

Dr. Kerry Magro, *Ed.D., CAS*

"*What's Your Anxiety Level? Cognitive Behavioral Therapy for Neurodivergent Children and Teens with Co-Occurring Anxiety Disorders* provides a voice for individuals, presenting activities that can be utilized across environments, empowering them to develop strong self-regulation skills as they take control of their emotions."

Carol Burmeister, *MA,*
Author and Educational Consultant

"When I worked with special education children and teens, I wished there had been a curriculum like Dr. Jennifer Cork's *What's Your Anxiety Level?* The cognitive behavioral therapy techniques which were successful with many populations did not resonate with our neurodivergent students or help them with their anxiety. Finally, now, we have answers and hope for these young people."

Wendela Whitcomb Marsh, *MA, RSD,*
Award-winning author of ten books on Autism

What's Your Anxiety Level? Cognitive Behavioral Therapy for Neurodivergent Children and Teens with Co-Occurring Anxiety Disorders

This book provides clinicians with a cognitive behavioral therapy (CBT)-informed curriculum specifically designed for neurodiverse children and teens with co-occurring anxiety disorders.

Research has shown that neurodivergent individuals respond better to mental health interventions when they are adapted to their unique needs. The concepts and strategies in this book, guided by CBT principles, address these needs and provide clinicians with an affirming and supportive approach to treatment with neurodiverse clients. The visually engaging templates throughout help clients recognize and communicate their feelings with others, allowing them to self-regulate and feel their emotions, leading to a sense of achievement during treatment.

A must-have resource on the bookshelf of any psychologist, social worker, counselor, and other professionals working with neurodivergent children and teens.

Dr. Jennifer Cork is an autistic Doctor of Social Work (DSW) and licensed Clinical Social Worker (LCSW). She specializes in treating neurodivergent children, teens, and adults, is a Certified Autism Specialist (CAS), ADHD-Certified Clinical Service Provider (ADHD-CCSP), and has a Graduate Certificate in Disability Studies.

What's Your Anxiety Level? Cognitive Behavioral Therapy for Neurodivergent Children and Teens with Co-Occurring Anxiety Disorders

Jennifer Cork

Routledge
Taylor & Francis Group

NEW YORK AND LONDON

Designed cover image: Getty Images © DrAfter123

First published 2026
by Routledge
605 Third Avenue, New York, NY 10158

and by Routledge
4 Park Square, Milton Park, Abingdon, Oxon, OX14 4RN

Routledge is an imprint of the Taylor & Francis Group, an informa business

© 2026 Jennifer Cork

ISBN: 978-1-041-01972-5 (hbk)
ISBN: 978-1-041-01975-6 (pbk)
ISBN: 978-1-003-61718-1 (ebk)

DOI: 10.4324/9781003617181

Typeset in Sabon
by Apex CoVantage, LLC

This book is dedicated to Tim, my husband, best friend, and neurodivergent opposite. You not only believed in me and saw my potential, but encouraged me to reach toward goals well beyond what we would have thought was possible at the age of 17. Without you, this book would not exist. I am happy to continue doing a good portion of your scheduling and organizing and to have you help me prep for social interactions and navigate changes in my plans.

Contents

Acknowledgments

I want to start out by again thanking my husband Tim, who encouraged me for years to complete this project. Next, I would like to thank our three kids who not only lived through mom needing space to work on this project, but on both my master's and doctoral degrees, as well as Dad's master's degree. All three of you are amazing and we can't wait to see what you accomplish as you leave the nest.

Next, I want to thank Tara Karr Roberts, journalist, professor, writer of fiction, editor, second cousin, and the first baby I was allowed to hold by myself other than my brother. I appreciate the hours you spent reviewing this project, which started in the last two semesters of my doctoral program. I especially appreciate your bearing with me during that last semester when I called you panicking because I had to start over with a new capstone project. I am also grateful for your pep talk, telling me to stop sending you my work and to trust myself and my new editors once my book proposal was accepted.

Thank you to two fantastic mentors who helped me to figure out the process of approaching publishers and navigate a system with which I was completely unfamiliar. First, Carol Burmeister, who has been a supporter and cheerleader since she approached me at an event celebrating the anniversary of the Americans with Disabilities Act after recently moving to the same area and hearing about my advocacy work. Your faith in me, including inviting me to write a chapter in the book, *Life After Lockdown: Resetting Perceptions of Autism*, was one of the confidence boosters that I needed. I appreciate your availability to answer questions about the publishing world, as well as your feedback about my finished project. Next, Dr. Wendela Witcomb Marsh, whom I met by chance at a coffee get-together for local therapists. I am especially grateful for your advice to read the book *Nonfiction Book Proposals Anybody Can Write: How to Get a Contract and Advance Before Writing Your Book*. I knew nothing about submitting book proposals and this recommendation was golden. I am also grateful for your support and availability to answer questions.

Finally, I want to thank all of the wonderful, neurodivergent kids, teens, and adults whom I have worked with over the last 20 years. I am honored to have been part of your journey, to learn with you, to help you problem solve, to self-advocate, and to grow. I appreciate your trust in me and feel that I learned as much from each of you as you did from me. Without you, this book would not exist.

Introduction

Note on the Language

While there is some debate in the neurodivergent community about whether to use identity-first or person-first language, identity-first language is the term currently preferred by a majority of self-advocates, especially by autistic individuals (Price, 2022). For this reason, and in order to respect the value of "nothing about us without us" (Autism Self Advocacy Network, n.d.), this curriculum will use identity-first language when referring to autistic people. Additionally, and also in line with terminology preferred by the majority of self-advocates, "autism spectrum disorder" will be referred to as "autism" (Price, 2022). Terminology preferences for attention-deficit/hyperactivity disorder, or ADHD, are a little less defined by the community, and there are no easy alternatives to use of the word "disorder" in the ADHD diagnosis. This curriculum will work to be affirming and use the term ADHD. Similarly, affirming language for individuals with intellectual disabilities is less defined, and this community tends to prefer person-first language (Hartman et al., 2023). Because of these preferences, this curriculum will work to be affirming and use "children with intellectual disabilities" or "children with ID." For those working with the neurodivergent population, it is important to check in with each individual and honor the ways in which they would like to be referred. For terms related to interests in the autism population, there is agreement among the community to avoid the use of the deficit-based language in the Diagnostic and Statistical Manual of Mental Disorders (DSM), but there is debate as to what more affirming language should be used (Hartman et al., 2023). This curriculum will use "special interests," as this is the language that I prefer as an autistic adult. Many autistic individuals, however, prefer the word "passion."

DOI: 10.4324/9781003617181-1

Curriculum Purpose

The Origins of This Curriculum

When I started my master of social work degree in 2011, I had been working with children receiving special education in the schools, and later with children receiving disability supports in my state of residence. I knew that after graduation, I wanted to continue to work with the neurodivergent community as I transitioned to the mental health setting. As learning itself is a special interest and I was used to relying on research as a first-generation college student to figure out things that I did not know, I began a deep dive into the research on what the best interventions for treatment for neurodivergent individuals with co-occurring mental health diagnoses would be. I found there were very few treatment resources available, little research on the intersectionality of neurodivergence and mental health, and few, if any, evidence-based treatment modalities for this population. The limited research that I did manage to find at the time pointed to cognitive behavioral therapy (CBT) as the most promising intervention for the neurodivergent community, although this was often the only modality being researched. With nothing else to go on, I focused on learning as much about CBT as I could in my internship and studies. Again, as learning is a special interest, I also researched alternative perspectives to behaviorism, such as the work of Dr. Dan Siegel and Dr. Ross Green, and psychoanalysts coming from a more humanistic lens such as Dr. Viktor Frankel and Dr. Irvin Yalom. While CBT and the routine and concreteness of steps spoke to me, so did those who called attention to the limitations of this modality and the theories behind it.

When I completed my degree and began working in mental health, I did not set out to create a CBT curriculum. However, with no other real resources to work with, especially when working with individuals with higher support needs, I took what I had learned in my studies during my master's program, along with what I had learned while working on my bachelor's degree of elementary education to create interventions and supports for my clients. My training in education taught me many tools and strategies for teaching, including learning theories, learning styles (which were popular in the early 2000s), and concepts such as scaffolding and adjusting instruction for diverse learners. These played a key role in my therapy work. As word got out in my community that I was a therapist with a background in working with neurodiverse children and teens, I received a flood of neurodivergent clients of all ages.

As I worked to treat these clients, I found that many were facing similar mental health struggles. Most of the neurodivergent and anxious children and teens who were being referred to me struggled with a combination of difficulties with emotional regulation and impulse control, exacerbated by anxiety, which often looked like anger. These children were anxious, but the systems in which they lived were not recognizing that their struggles were related to mental health; therefore, they were not getting the specific tools and supports they needed. Most of the children were, as Dr. Ross Greene (2010) describes it, lagging in executive functioning skills when it came to emotional regulation. These children and teens needed extra support to learn about what they were feeling, how to communicate those feelings to others (think Dr. Siegel's (2011) "Name it to Tame it"), and to manage those feelings by increasing their ability to self-regulate in healthy ways. I took what I had studied in my master's program, as well as in my bachelor's of education, and found interventions that really worked. As I developed tools for clients, using my experience working in multiple systems, including education and disability services, I worked to ensure that they would be applicable for kids and teens throughout the systems in which they were involved. I wanted to make sure that these tools were accessible to the individual, whether the person was at home, at school, doing extracurricular activities, or participating in other treatment services. Because of my own undiagnosed autism and reliance on routines, I presented these interventions to clients the same way, in the same order, and realized that I had developed my own CBT intervention. This intervention, or curriculum, included a few simple concepts and tools designed to help children and their caregivers better understand themselves and learn ways to more effectively self-regulate.

As I began implementing this curriculum, I found that my clients, with the help of their parents as coaches, quickly got better at self-regulation and managing their anxiety. After I had used this curriculum for five years with dozens of clients of all ages, my husband encouraged me to seek publication so that my methods could be used by others. Running into a case of imposter syndrome, I felt that this would be very presumptuous of me. He continued to encourage me, and I eventually decided to pursue a doctor of social work degree. I felt that having "doctor" in front of my name would help me move past my impostor syndrome and also help me improve my curriculum. I worked to further my studies, which allowed me not only to further develop my curriculum utilizing the latest research but also to understand my own methods and better articulate my work so that the curriculum could be fully understood and utilized by other mental health professionals.

In the course of my doctoral studies, I also focused on researching more about neurodivergent women, girls, and those who do not fall into a binary gender category. Through this research, along with treating more neurodivergent women who were professionals like myself, I realized that the reason I felt so comfortable in the neurodivergent community was because

I was autistic. I received an official diagnosis during the last semester of my doctoral program. Looking back, I can see that I myself was an autistic child and teen with severe anxiety that was missed because a majority of my symptoms of anxiety were internalized, rather than externalized, which is a common experience for neurodivergent individuals, especially women and girls.

My hope in creating and sharing this curriculum is to raise awareness of this underserved population's needs and to help the mental health profession better support neurodivergent children and teens who struggle with co-occurring anxiety. The ultimate goal of this curriculum, as well as my own practice as an autistic doctor of social work, is to help the mental health system support neurodivergent children receive the understanding and support that they need to thrive.

Why Is This Curriculum Needed?

Co-occurring mental health diagnoses are frequent in the neurodivergent population. As many as 70% of autistic people qualify for at least one mental health diagnosis, and 50% qualify for two or more (Lai et al., 2019). Anxiety disorders are common in this population, especially in children, and it is estimated that as many as 40–50% of autistic children have co-occurring anxiety disorders (Driscoll et al., 2020; Guzick et al., 2022; Hollocks et al., 2022; McBride et al., 2020; Ramirez et al., 2020; Sharma et al., 2021; Solish et al., 2020; Wang et al., 2021). For those with ADHD, about 78% qualify for at least one mental health diagnosis, including high rates of behavioral diagnoses such as conduct disorder (CD) and oppositional defiant disorder (ODD), as well as high rates of anxiety and depressive disorders (Centers for Disease Control and Prevention, 2024). For those with intellectual disabilities, the research is less clear, but it is widely accepted that about 35% of individuals have a co-occurring mental health diagnosis (National Association for the Dually Diagnosed, n.d.). Despite this high rate of co-occurrence, one study found that only 10% of individuals with ID had accessed mental health services compared to 35% of the general population (Sauter et al., 2023).

Unfortunately, the current mental health system is not equipped to meet the needs of the neurodivergent community. Very few mental health therapists are trained to treat this population (Cantor et al., 2020). For example, a recent study found that while there is a need for mental health therapy for autistic children, there are few therapists who are available to address this need. After surveying more than 8,000 mental health clinics in the United States, researchers reported that only 43% would accept a referral for a child with an autism diagnosis. Of that 43%, only 12.7% had a therapist with any training or experience in treating autistic children, and only 4.3% had therapists using treatment interventions specifically designed for autistic children (Cantor et al., 2020). For those with ADHD, research has found that traits of ADHD are often not addressed by mental health professionals. This is problematic because for many individuals, their traits of ADHD are the primary cause of their anxiety and depression (Arellano-Virto et al., 2021; Young et al., 2020). Therefore, in not addressing the potential challenges associated with ADHD, the therapists are only addressing secondary causes and not the primary causes of the person's struggles with mental health. This is especially true for women and girls with ADHD, who are more likely to go undiagnosed as their traits of ADHD are missed due to much of the research focusing on males and male presentations of this diagnosis (Young et al., 2020). For individuals with intellectual disabilities, the system has only recognized relatively recently that this group of individuals can experience struggles with mental health. Often, behaviors deemed "problematic" by society were and still are associated with the person's disability, rather than a mental health concern (Sauter et al., 2023). Studies have found that individuals with intellectual disabilities have a hard time accessing mental healthcare, that mental health professionals struggle to adequately meet their unique therapeutic needs, and that these individuals are more likely to be hospitalized for mental health struggles than the general population (Sauter et al., 2023; Lineberry et al., 2023). This is likely why only 10% of individuals with ID are accessing mental healthcare (Sauter et al., 2023).

Additionally, there are few evidence-based interventions for treating individuals with co-occurring neurodevelopmental disabilities and mental health diagnoses. Among modalities that are currently recommended as promising for treating neurodivergent individuals, there are few interventions available created specifically for this population. Of these interventions, most were published more than five years ago. Additionally, after a thorough search of the resources available, none identified were created for autistic children with higher support needs or who have intellectual disabilities (Kilburn et al., 2023; Perihan et al., 2020; Solish et al., 2020; Sze & Wood, 2008).

These problems greatly impact the neurodivergent population. The combination of the high rates of mental health diagnoses, the lack of evidence-based treatment interventions, and the lack of trained mental health professionals who are competent in treating neurodivergent children and adolescents means that many are either going without care, or being treated by individuals who do not fully understand the intersectionality of neurodiversity and mental health (Cantor et al., 2020). This is problematic because untreated or ineffectively treated anxiety disorders lead to long-term negative outcomes (Fuselier et al., 2023; Jones et al., 2022). These negative outcomes include increased risk of poor mental health, higher rates of self-harm, suicidality, externalized behaviors, difficulties with completing activities of daily living, struggles in education, and in future employment settings (Fuselier et al., 2023; Jones et al., 2022; McBride et al., 2020; Perihan et al., 2020; Solish et al., 2020).

Why Cognitive Behavioral Therapy?

Cognitive behavioral therapy (CBT) utilizes two theories: cognitive theory and behavioral theory. Cognitive theory focuses on the ways in which a person's thoughts influence the way they feel and behave. If one is struggling with negative thoughts, they are more likely to feel negative and behave in unhelpful ways. By identifying and changing negative thought patterns, a person can change the way they feel and behave in more positive ways (Payne, 2020). Similarly, behavioral theory explores the ways in which behaviors can influence one's thoughts and feelings. If one has unhealthy or maladaptive behaviors, it will have a negative effect on the ways in which the person thinks and feels. If one can find more healthy and adaptive behaviors, it will have a positive effect on thoughts and feelings. Behavioral theory also explores the ways in which one's environment affects behavior and how it may even be reinforcing those unhelpful behaviors (Early & Grady, 2017; Payne, 2020).

Cognitive and behavioral theories are combined in this curriculum to create a CBT curriculum that addresses both unhealthy behaviors and thoughts about those unhealthy behaviors that are often the result of anxiety. Many neurodivergent children with mental health disorders struggle with either externalized behaviors or internalized behaviors. Externalized behaviors may include irritability, difficulty concentrating, or meltdowns. Internalized behaviors may include dissociation, trouble concentrating, stomach aches, and shut downs. These types of behaviors are often attributed to the individual's disability, when in fact they are a result of mental health struggles associated with anxiety and/or depression (Lineberry et al., 2023; Sauter et al., 2023). When others mistake the source of the behaviors, they often do not address the behaviors in a way that would be most helpful to the individual (Jones et al., 2022; McBride et al., 2020; Sauter et al., 2023). This is problematic because if left untreated, anxiety disorders can cause long-term difficulties for neurodivergent children (Driscoll et al., 2020; Fuselier et al., 2023; Jones et al., 2022; McBride et al., 2020; Perihan et al., 2020; Solish et al., 2020).

This CBT curriculum does not focus on which diagnosis causes the externalized or internalized behaviors, but, instead, focuses on first helping the individual to recognize and communicate what emotions they are feeling to others, and then giving them healthy ways to manage and process those feelings. Additionally, this curriculum presents an alternate way of thinking about the externalized and internalized behaviors. Many neurodivergent children struggling with externalized behaviors are treated as though they are "bad kids" with "problem behaviors." This curriculum teaches that these behaviors are not negative or "bad," but are related to an instinctive fight, flight, or freeze response. In other words, the behaviors stem from anxiety and the person's subsequent stress response. Once the behavior is reframed in this way, the focus is on finding healthy versus unhealthy ways to engage in one's natural stress responses. In this way, neurodivergent children are empowered to work on their anxiety through increased strategies to self-regulate. Simultaneously, they are given permission to feel their emotions and act on them, rather than on having to focus on behavior management. Another way to think of this is that the goal of the curriculum is to address the ways in which anxiety is affecting the neurodivergent individual and how to give them effective supports to process and manage their anxiety – not to focus on the ways in which the individual's behavior is a problem that needs to be extinguished because it is negatively affecting the people around them.

In order to ensure that this curriculum is accessible to diverse learners, the concepts introduced are concrete and focused on teaching just a few concepts in the first few weeks. There are accommodations for each tool as well, in recognition that there is no one-size-fits-all intervention. The remainder of treatment is focused on reinforcing and practicing these concepts in ways that are backed up in the research and also meet each individual's unique needs. If the person is able to go more deeply into CBT concepts, there is room for this, but, if not, focus should be on the following:

1. Recognizing and communicating one's feelings
2. Finding healthy ways to act on those feelings (healthy stress responses)
3. Rethinking the struggles the individual is having with self-regulation as a symptom of anxiety, rather than a "problem behavior"

Cognitive Behavioral Therapy for Autistic Children

It is important to note that CBT is not a therapy for Autism, but for the co-occurring mental health diagnosis, in this case, anxiety. While CBT has not achieved the status of evidence-based treatment for autistic children with anxiety disorders, current research shows that autistic children respond well to CBT interventions. However, research also reflects that interventions should be adapted to meet the unique needs of this population in order to increase its efficacy (Hollocks et al., 2022; Jones et al., 2022; Kilburn et al., 2023; McBride et al., 2020; Solish et al., 2020; Sze & Wood, 2008; Wood et al., 2020). Adaptations based on current research have informed the development of this curriculum and will be outlined below.

Cognitive Behavioral Therapy for Children with ADHD

Again, it is important to note that while there are CBT curricula for addressing executive functioning challenges associated with ADHD, those curricula are evidence-based for adults, not for children or teens. For children and adolescents with ADHD, CBT interventions such as this one, which targets self-regulation, are recommended. Note, however, that the available research in this area is still limited. CBT interventions for ADHD should address the difficulties with emotional regulation and impulse control that are often experienced by this population. Early cognitive training that focuses on emotional regulation, as early as the preschool years, has been shown to minimize struggles with externalized behaviors in individuals with ADHD (Pauli-Pott et al., 2021). Additionally, it is frequently recommended that parents receive education about ADHD, which will help them better understand and support their child (Centers for Disease Control and Prevention, 2019; Meyer et al., 2022). Clinicians treating this population should incorporate psychoeducation about ADHD as part of their overall treatment.

Cognitive Behavioral Therapy for Intellectually Disabled Children

CBT is not a therapy to treat ID, but again, is for the co-occurring anxiety disorder that the person with ID is struggling with. Many of the studies that were reviewed for this curriculum excluded children with ID (Kilburn et al., 2023; Perihan et al., 2020; Robe & Dobrean, 2023; Solish et al., 2020; Sze & Wood, 2008). The exclusion of these children occurs frequently in clinical trials due to methodological barriers for ethical inclusion of this population (Sauter et al., 2023). Additionally, many of the existing CBT curricula created for neurodivergent children are not intended or developmentally appropriate for children with ID (Kilburn et al., 2023; Perihan et al., 2020; Solish et al., 2020; Sauter et al., 2023; Sze & Wood, 2008). Despite these barriers, there is emerging research showing that CBT that has been adapted for individuals with ID can be an effective treatment intervention (Sauter et al., 2023). This curriculum was created using learning theories that support diverse learners, including those with ID.

Criticisms of CBT for Neurodivergent Children

As stated earlier, there are few evidence-based interventions for treating mental health diagnoses in autistic children. This has led to debates within the autistic and mental health communities due to the lack of clarity regarding what treatment modalities are efficacious and should be utilized in treatment. For example, CBT has been found to be effective for treating anxiety disorders in neurotypical children, or children who are developing within what is considered to be the norm, without meeting the criteria for a learning or neurodevelopmental disability. CBT for neurodivergent children, or those who are developing outside of what is considered to be the norm, has been questioned by advocates and mental health professionals with regard to its efficacy. A recent example of this is a book written by an autistic clinical psychologist which states twice that CBT may not be as effective for autistic people as it is for neurotypical people, citing two articles to make this case (Price, 2022). Due to the author being both a professional and autistic, these statements about CBT are powerful and should be duly noted. However, by only using two articles, these statements do not fully account for what current research has found regarding the use of CBT with autistic individuals. This may then lead to clinicians not using a potentially beneficial intervention to treat autistic clients, or may lead clinicians who primarily utilize CBT to not accept autistic clients in their therapy practices.

When looking more closely at what the literature has to say about the effectiveness of CBT for neurodivergent children with anxiety disorders, it is true that research has found that traditional CBT interventions are less effective for autistic children compared to the general population. However, while the research showed fewer benefits, it did not find that there were no benefits to CBT interventions, but just that the benefits were smaller (Driscoll et al., 2020; Guzick et al., 2022; Hollocks et al., 2022; McBride et al., 2020; Perihan et al., 2020; Pickard et al., 2020; Sharma et al., 2021; Solish et al., 2020; Wang et al., 2021; Wood et al., 2020). Research also reflects that while traditional CBT may have some benefit, CBT interventions specifically tailored for neurodivergent children were found to be more effective (Hollocks et al., 2022; Jones et al., 2022; Kilburn et al., 2023; McBride et al., 2020; Solish et al., 2020; Sze & Wood, 2008; Wood et al., 2020). It is important to look more closely, as the literature is also clear that not treating anxiety in neurodivergent children can have a number of long-term ill effects (Fuselier et al., 2023; Jones et al., 2022; McBride et al., 2020; Perihan et al., 2020; Solish et al., 2020). Currently, the literature seems to reflect that CBT is a promising intervention for treating anxiety disorders in neurodivergent children, but that the CBT should be modified to account for the intersectionality of mental health and neurodiversity in order to fully meet the needs of autistic children.

Because the literature also reflects that very few mental health therapists have training and expertise in treating neurodivergent children, and even fewer are using interventions created specifically for them (Cantor et al., 2020), it is reasonable to conclude that CBT may not be the problem. Instead of CBT being ineffective, it is likely that the CBT that neurodivergent individuals are receiving has not been properly adapted. It is also likely that the CBT neurodivergent individuals are receiving is not being provided by professionals who understand their autism, ADHD, and/or ID and how those disabilities intersect and interact with their mental health.

CBT Adaptations for Neurodivergent Children Found in This Curriculum

Use of Adaptive Learning Tools

This curriculum utilizes adaptive learning tools to help reinforce concepts. These adaptive learning tools include increased use of visuals, use of multiple learning styles to introduce topics, use of concrete concepts, and using interventions for developmental age, rather than chronological age, while still working to respect the individual's chronological age (Driscoll et al., 2020; Guzick et al., 2022; Pickard et al., 2020; Sauter et al., 2023; Sze & Wood, 2008). This is done through the use of the Universal Design for Learning (UDL) educational framework. The UDL framework works to create equity in learning by presenting lesson content in a variety of ways in order to reach a variety of learners (Gannon, 2020). This curriculum will utilize this framework by ensuring that each concept introduced is accessible to individuals from a variety of learning styles and adapted specifically for their needs. For example, when utilizing a Likert scale to measure emotion, which is common in CBT interventions, this curriculum will use the model from *The Incredible 5-Point Scale,* which uses numbers, colors, pictures, and spatial interventions to emphasize the content (Buron & Curtis, 2022). Therapists who are unfamiliar with UDL would benefit from researching this framework before administering this curriculum. For more information, a good place to start is CAST, a nonprofit educational research organization that developed the UDL framework. Their website is: https://www.cast.org.

Scaffolding and Repetition of Concepts

CBT interventions for neurodivergent children that utilize scaffolding or introducing concepts one at a time that build on each other have been shown to help increase treatment efficacy. The individual should then practice these skills until they are able to use them independently (Meyer et al., 2022; Pauli-Pott et al., 2021). To achieve this, the curriculum utilizes repetition of concepts to help aid neurodivergent children who struggle with difficulties in generalizing skills, processing verbal language and other types of information, or working memory (Driscoll et al., 2020; Pickard et al., 2020). Participants will be given just a few, basic concepts in the beginning of treatment, and then will spend the remainder of treatment receiving time and space to review and practice concepts both in sessions and through daily homework practice supported by parents. This adaptation is also in line with the UDL framework.

Incorporating Special Interests

The use of special interests will help increase interest and engagement and help make tools more meaningful for each individual. The importance of incorporating special interests for autistic children has been shown to be especially important when adapting CBT interventions (Cho et al., 2023; Fuselier et al., 2023; Lake et al., 2020; McBride et al., 2020; Perihan et al., 2020; Storch et al., 2022; Sze & Wood, 2008; Wood et al., 2020). Using special interests will help autistic children establish rapport with their therapist, increase motivation, and increase understanding of concepts because the information will be connected with a topic they are already interested in. Using special interests for other neurodivergent children, such as those with ADHD and ID, will help make the content more relatable, engaging, and meaningful. This curriculum is unique, in that each CBT tool is individualized as it is created in session with the child and incorporates the child's special interests. For example, when creating a 5-point anger scale using the template from *The Incredible 5-Point Scale* (Buron & Curtis, 2022), the child will first identify each level of anger with a character from a favorite show, game, or other topic. For examples, refer to Sessions 1–3 provided here.

Inclusion of Caregivers in Treatment

The final adaptation used in this curriculum is the full inclusion of parents. Multiple studies have explored the use of parents in treatment, and each found that neurodivergent children did significantly better when parents were involved (Meyer et al., 2022; Perihan et al., 2020; Wood et al., 2020). Caregiver involvement is helpful because it leads to the caregiver having an increased understanding of their child, teaches them helpful strategies to support their child, and ensures that caregivers know specific tools to use to prompt their child in moments of anxiety. Caregiver involvement also has been shown to increase the child's generalization of skills, to reduce externalized behaviors, and to lead to more effective adaptations to curricula, as caregivers know their children best and so are more able to help treatment providers identify effective adaptations (Byrne et al., 2023; Jones et al., 2022; Driscoll et al., 2020; Ramirez et al., 2020). Parental involvement may also increase motivation and treatment adherence (Meyer et al., 2022) and may also lead to continued reduction of anxiety symptoms after treatment has ended. For example, Driscoll et al. (2020) showed moderate progress for a group of children who received parent-led CBT, with 40% of participants no longer meeting qualifications for their primary anxiety disorder diagnoses after treatment. However, after a four-month follow-up, researchers reported that gains had continued, with 82% of the children no longer meeting qualifications for their anxiety disorder diagnosis. Driscoll et al. (2020) felt that this indicated that parents had continued to do the CBT work with their children after treatment ended and reflects the benefits of giving autistic children more time for practice and repetition in order to more fully generalize skills.

Additionally, research shows that caregivers report benefits for themselves. These benefits include improved awareness of their child's emotions, and that they personally feel more cared for and more supported in the mental healthcare system (Byrne et al., 2023; Jones et al., 2022; Driscoll et al., 2020; Ramirez et al., 2020). Another benefit of caregiver involvement is that it decreases family accommodation of anxiety. Family accommodation, which includes behaviors caregivers engage in to reduce their child's anxiety in the moment, can actually lead to increased anxiety over time. Family accommodation is a common behavior found in families where children, both neurotypical and neurodiverse, are struggling with anxiety disorders. While it is common, this behavior is a barrier to progress in treatment, as the caregiver may inadvertently reinforce behaviors such as avoidance, which can increase anxiety long term (Byrne et al., 2023). Overall, current research reflects that the inclusion of parents in CBT interventions should be a standard adaptation for neurodivergent children. Additionally, there are instructions in the curriculum about how to facilitate coordination of care with other providers, as this is important to help facilitate the success of treatment for the child.

Social Skills Supports

Research has found that the inclusion of social skills training is beneficial in adapted CBT interventions, as differences in social interactions can increase anxiety for autistic children (Driscoll et al., 2020; McBride et al., 2020). There are a number of social skills training interventions for autistic children. However, in line with the social model of disability, it is important to note that social skills training is often seen by the autistic community as unaffirming and an effort to make autistic children present as neurotypical children (Penot, 2024; Price, 2022; Silberman, 2015). Instead of social skills training, this curriculum encourages therapists to approach neurodivergence as its own community and culture, and to use a more humanistic approach in building social skills through the therapy relationship.

There is, of course, some irony of a CBT curriculum encouraging the use of humanistic approaches, as humanistic theory was developed as an alternative to behavioral theories. However, when approaching social skills supports for neurodivergent children through the framework of the social model of disability, the goal is not to change the way the child socializes in order to make them present as neurotypical, but to help build skills that will enable the person to meet their own social goals and to minimize anxiety in social situations. Humanistic theories encourage a person-centered approach to therapy in which the therapist works to develop unconditional positive regard toward their client. While developing this regard, the therapist also works to present their true self to the client, rather than a persona meant to influence. The therapist also works to emphasize the client's perception of the world. In humanism, the person is the expert on their lives and they are empowered to make changes and to work toward self-improvement and self-actualization on their own terms. In order to accomplish this, the work is done primarily through the human relationship with the therapist, who again is presenting an authentic self to the client (Payne, 2020).

In using this approach, the therapist should follow the child's lead and focus on building a relationship, not on making the child adhere to neurotypical social norms. The focus is on the concept of reciprocity. This means that communication and social interactions should include give-and-take from both parties (Gernsbacher, 2006). Neurotypical therapists should approach social skills training with cultural humility when treating autistic children, just as they would if they were working with any other community of which they were not a member. Through this process, both the child and the clinician will gain social skills and competency in interacting with the other's culture, that is, neurodivergent versus neurotypical cultures. Neurodivergent therapists should focus on the give-and-take of the relationship, just as they would with a neurodivergent peer, although keeping in mind age differences and professional boundaries. Through this reciprocal relationship, both parties will likely gain not just social skills, but the joy of connection with another human being as well. For more on the use of this technique, see the content in Sessions 6–9.

Can This Curriculum Be Used With Neurotypical Children?

As society has worked to make systems more accessible for the disability population, we have found that those reasonable accommodations and adaptations benefit nondisabled individuals as well. For example, when the Americans with Disabilities Act (ADA) of 1990 mandated that all sidewalks needed to have a curb cut or ramp to make them more accessible for wheelchair users, Americans found that these were very useful for strollers, shopping carts, bicycles, and other wheeled objects (Mackelprang et al., 2021). The same is true for accommodations and adaptations. In using the UDL framework to inform this curriculum, the goal is to make it more accessible to anyone because each and every one of us has a unique brain.

Social Model of Disability and How It Informs This Curriculum

Historically, interventions and therapies for neurodiverse children, especially autistic children, have been focused on making them more "normal" (Penot, 2024; Price, 2022; Silberman, 2015). Because of this, it is important that any treatment intervention created for the neurodivergent community be anti-ableist and is one of the primary goals and purposes of this curriculum. To work toward this goal, the social model of disability will be utilized. The social model of disability conceives of disability both as an important characteristic of human diversity and as a social construct created by a society that does not adequately understand or provide adaptations that the disabled individual requires in order to succeed (Gibson et al., 2021; Hartman et al., 2023; Mackelprang et al., 2021). This CBT curriculum utilizes the social model of disability through adaptations such as individualizing CBT tools for each child and allowing them to personalize visuals. Along with choosing themes based on their special interests, therapists will work to use the child's own language to describe concepts and will facilitate the child in choosing their own potential coping skills. The clinician will ensure that these coping skills are healthy, rather than unhealthy, but the child will have a final say in what works for them. Most importantly, this curriculum will emphasize the child's right to say no and will encourage adults, including the clinician, caregivers, or anyone else in the child's natural support system, to allow the children to negotiate and make choices for themselves. The overall goal of this curriculum is to support mental wellness, not to change anyone or make them less neurodivergent.

Intersectionality

Intersectionality is a term coined by Kimberlé Crenshaw to explain that individuals may have multiple identities, which may cause them to be part of the majority or minority, or have varying experiences, depending on the setting in which they find themselves (Daftary, 2018). This curriculum directly addresses children who are in the intersection of neurodivergence and mental health challenges by acknowledging that these two identities are not separate. Unfortunately because of the ways current systems work, neurodivergent children often receive therapies to address their disability from professionals with little knowledge of mental health. If they are able to access mental health therapy, these professionals often have limited knowledge of the child's neurodivergence. When treating a neurodivergent child in the mental health system, it is important to recognize that both diagnoses equally contribute to the issues that brought the child in for treatment. Professionals should take time to gain competency in order to address any intersectionalities that make up the child's identity.

It is also important to note when adding additional, intersectional identities, this means that the child or teen will likely face increased adversities (Price, 2022). Therapists should consider the individuals' multiple identities and how this may impact them in their daily lives when providing treatment. These intersectionalities may include gender, gender identity, sexuality, race, and ethnicity. Each of these identities makes up the whole person and should be considered in treatment interventions.

Gender and Gender Identity

There is a growing recognition in the research on how gender and gender identity affect neurodivergent individuals. Much of the research on neurodevelopmental disabilities has focused on boys, so the current understanding of these diagnoses is focused on how they present in males. Because of this, women, girls, and genderdiverse individuals are often missed, or receive diagnoses at much later ages than their male peers. For example, Current CDC data reflect that four times as many boys as girls are diagnosed with autism (Centers for Disease Control and Prevention, 2025). Many in the autism community question this statistic because researchers historically only focused on male subjects (Price, 2022; Silberman, 2015). This means that the data collected reflected what autism looks like in boys, but not what it looked like in girls. This has led to higher rates of boys being diagnosed, which means that assessments, such as the Autism Diagnostic Observation Schedule – Second Edition (ADOS-2), which is considered the gold standard for diagnosing Autism in children, was normed for traits of autism typically seen in cis-gender boys. Because of this, it is likely that current autism testing is less effective at identifying autism in non-males, meaning that many girls go undiagnosed, or get diagnosed at later ages. This leads to an increase in social difficulties, without understanding the reasons (Freeman & Grigoriadis, 2023). The focus of research on autistic males also negatively affects individuals who do not fit into traditional gender binaries. This is a problem because autistic people are much more likely to identify as genderdiverse compared to the general population. A recent study, for example, found that transgender individuals were 3–6% more likely to also be diagnosed with autism than the general population (Weir et al., 2021).

Similarly, women and girls with ADHD are often overlooked and undiagnosed. According to data from the Centers for Disease Control and Prevention (2024), boys are diagnosed at a rate of 15% and girls at a rate of 8%. Research has shown that this is not due to ADHD being a predominantly male disorder, but is more likely due to a failure of recognizing ADHD in females (Young et al., 2020). This is likely due to males with ADHD being more likely to present with external symptoms, while females are more likely to have internalized symptoms (Katzman et al., 2017; Young et al., 2020). For these reasons, it is important to understand the intersectionality of ADHD in females and how this may influence their mental health needs.

Sexuality

This intersectionality is especially impactful for the autism community. Autistic individuals are much more likely to identify as LGBTQ+ than the general population. Autistic men are more likely to be gay or bi-sexual compared to neurotypical men and autistic women are more likely to identify as gay or lesbian than neurotypical women. Autistic individuals are 8.1 times more likely to identify as asexual and 7.6 times more likely to identify their sexuality as "other," or not easily defined compared to their non-autistic peers. Autistic adults are less likely to identify as heterosexual than neurotypicals (Weir et al., 2021). While children may not be fully aware of their sexuality, older children and teens will start to explore this. Clinicians should be aware of this intersectionality, as many individuals need support as they explore their sexuality.

Race and Ethnicity

The intersection of neurodivergence with race and ethnicity is important to acknowledge, as many minorities face additional adversities and challenges compared to their white peers. For example, research has shown that black parents bring up developmental concerns with their child's pediatricians at the same ages as white parents, but black children tend to receive Autism diagnoses at older ages, are more likely to be misdiagnosed with things such as conduct disorders, and are less likely to receive support services than their white peers (Dababnah et al., 2018; Mandell et al., 2007; Miller et al., 2023). Another example is that research has found that many racial and ethnic minority populations are less likely to engage with ADHD treatments due to distrust of the medical community and the long history of racism within these systems (Kamimura-Nishimura et al., 2023.

Because of this history, many children are going without treatments like talk therapy or medication therapies that may be helpful. Mental health professionals must be aware of how intersecting identities may impact their client and their client's mental health, due to the presence of racism and other biases within systems. Professionals must be aware of how race and ethnic can impact individuals, ensure cultural humility, and take time to listen to parents' concerns and to give quality information and education to families.

Brief Review of the Guiding Principles of This CBT Curriculum

1. **Goals of the curriculum.** In line with the social model of disability, the goal of this curriculum is to help give neurodivergent children and teens tools in order to help them better understand themselves, to more effectively manage their anxiety, and to gain more effective and healthy self-regulation tools.

2. **What is NOT the goal of the curriculum?** Also, in line with the social model of disability, it is **not** the goal of this curriculum to treat the child or adolescent's neurodivergence in order to make them more "normal." Neurodivergence is what makes them unique and each individual should be valued and celebrated for their uniqueness.

3. **Focus first on building a relationship.** A trusting relationship is one of the most important factors in determining the success of a therapy intervention (Norcross & Lambert, 2018). Kids and teens should enjoy coming to therapy and engaging in treatment. The best way to ensure that this happens is to ensure that they like you. Have fun, be silly, get on the floor, and be real and genuine with clients. They deserve a treatment provider who genuinely cares for and likes them.

4. **This is a judgment-free zone.** The children that come for treatment are likely struggling with many behaviors that have been labeled "difficult" or "problematic" by their parents, teachers, and other community members. These behaviors will likely include meltdowns, shut downs, verbal and physical aggression, and other things that can feel stressful for those around them. Therapy should be a place where they can talk about these anxiety behaviors without judgment. They get plenty of judgment from society, they do not need judgment from their therapist. Ensure that you hear the information, give a neutral response, focus on what went well and what did not, and then on planning what support or strategy they need in the future that may have been missing.

5. **The therapist needs to stay regulated.** When working with this population, the anxiety behaviors outlined earlier are likely to occur in treatment at some point. It is important to stay regulated in order to avoid

co-dysregulation. We are all human, so keep in mind what things you need to do in order to keep yourself regulated, being mindful of your own stress responses. Remember not to personalize the child's behavior. While it may be directed at you, it is likely not about you, but about their anxiety.

6. **Children and teens are allowed to say "no" and their "no" should be respected.** Historically and currently in educational interventions and services for children with neurodevelopmental disabilities, there is an emphasis on "compliance." Because of this emphasis, children learn from a very young age to do what they are told without question by authority figures. Research has found that this emphasis on compliance has contributed to higher rates of victimization and abuse for neurodivergent children and adults (Pearson et al., 2023; Price, 2022). This is not that type of intervention. Any child or teen receiving CBT therapy should be allowed to say "no" and their "no" should be respected. This does not mean that the treatment provider is required to accept the "no" without question, but may mean a "plan B" discussion as per Dr. Ross Greene (2010). For more information about the emphasis on compliance and the potential, negative long-term effects, please see Session 1.

7. **Listen to your clients, ask questions, and believe what they tell you.** This may seem obvious, but it is common for adults to minimize or ignore what children say or dismiss their points of view. This is especially true for neurodivergent children as they often run into situations where they are misunderstood. They are also more likely to give push and to be labeled with oppositional defiant disorder (ODD) or with pervasive demand avoidance (PDA), which has been rebranded by autistic self-advocates as persistent desire for autonomy and other similar, more affirming labels. This is due to the fact that these children are living in a world that was not made for them, does not fully understand or accommodate them, and so they learn to push back. Because of this, their complaints or points of view are frequently ignored, dismissed, and discounted, which will harm the therapy relationship and prevent progress toward reaching the child's therapy goals. It also teaches the child not to bother self-advocating, which will lead to a more vulnerable individual.

8. **Ask questions.** Neurodivergent children are more likely to struggle with explaining their physical and emotional experiences. This is called alexithymia and this difficulty will increase as a person's emotional dysregulation increases (Eyler, 2018; Mazefsky & White, 2014; Siegel & Payne Bryson, 2011). Because of this, therapists will need to do some detective work, asking open-ended questions, sharing what

you think you hear, and being willing to receive the feedback that you heard wrong. This can sometimes be frustrating, especially for the child or teen who is struggling to articulate the difficulty they are having. Reassure them that you really want to understand their problem so that you can help them the right way. Also, have the awareness that some of the frustration may be related to the fact that the child has likely been criticized for this aspect of their disability. If frustration gets too high, save the discussion for the following week, making sure that they are open to talking about it again before revisiting the issue.

An example that stands out in my clinical work is a teen who was struggling with writing assignments. I made assumptions, based on my past experience with many clients over the years, that the issue was with task initiation, or organizing thoughts. I introduced a number of tools for this, including timers, schedules, and graphic organizers. The teen continued to get frustrated as they explained that none of this was the problem. After setting them up with an appointment with another professional who specialized in using graphic organizers, they finally found the words to explain that just the act of writing was the problem. I finally got it and took out the teen's 5-point anxiety scale. Together, we mapped out where different writing tasks fit on their scale. While all writing caused anxiety, writing facts was a 2 and writing poetry was a 5. It took four sessions to get to this point, but once I was able to understand the problem, I was able to help the teen tackle writing anxiety in a much more helpful way.

9. **If at first you don't succeed, try, try again!** If you have introduced a concept and the child did not understand it, this means that you need to find another approach to explain the information. This may also mean that the tool is too difficult and needs to be simplified, or it needs to be explained in smaller chunks. This curriculum includes many such adaptations, but spending time learning more about educational frameworks such as Universal Design for Learning is recommended to help diverse learners succeed in treatment.

10. **Continue to build cultural competence.** As Dr. Stephen Shore is often quoted, "If you've met one person with autism, you've met one person with autism." The same is true for ADHD, ID, and any other diagnosis. This is true even if you share the diagnosis yourself. Continue to talk and listen to neurodivergent people. Continue to research, study, and attend trainings on neurodiversity. Most importantly, in line with the philosophy of "Nothing about us without us," (Autism Self Advocacy Network, n.d.), make sure that you are reading books, articles, blog posts, TED Talks, and other content created by neurodivergent people.

Note on Treatment Examples

In order to illustrate concepts, the characters of Emily and James were created. These characters are fictional and not based on any clients seen by this author. Some examples are based on actual experiences with clients, but the information has been modified to protect privacy.

References

Arellano-Virto, P. T., Seubert-Ravelo, A. N., Prieto-Corona, B., Witt-González, A., & Yáñez-Téllez, G. (2021). Association between psychiatric symptoms and executive function in adults with attention deficit hyperactivity disorder. *Psychology & Neuroscience, 14*(4), 438–453. https://doi.org/10.1037/pne0000271

Autism Self Advocacy Network. (n.d.). *About ASAN.* Autism Self Advocacy Network. https://autisticadvocacy.org/about-asan/

Buron, K. D., & Curtis, M. (2022). *The incredible 5-point scale: Assisting students in understanding social interactions and controlling their emotional responses* (2nd ed.). 5 Point Scale Publishing.

Byrne, G., Ghráda, Á. N., & O'Mahony, T. (2023). Parent-led cognitive behavioural therapy for children with autism spectrum conditions. A pilot study. *Journal of Autism and Developmental Disorders, 53*(1), 263–274. https://doi.org/10.1007/s10803-022-05424-2

Cantor, J., McBain, R. K., Kofner, A., Stein, B. D., & Yu, H. (2020). Fewer than half of US mental health treatment facilities provide services for children with autism spectrum disorder. *Health Affairs, 39*(6), 968–974. https://doi.org/10.1377/hlthaff.2019.01557

Centers for Disease Control and Prevention. (2019). *Treatment of ADHD.* https://www.cdc.gov/ncbddd/adhd/treatment.html

Centers for Disease Control and Prevention. (2024). *Data and statistics on ADHD.* U.S. Department of Health & Human Services. https://www.cdc.gov/adhd/data/index.html

Centers for Disease Control and Prevention. (2025). *Data and statistics on autism spectrum disorder.* Department of Health & Human Services.

Cho, A., Wood, J. J., Ferrer, E., Rosenau, K., Storch, E. A., & Kendall, P. C. (2023). Empirically-identified subgroups of children with autism spectrum disorder and their response to two types of cognitive behavioral therapy. *Developmental Psychopathology, 35*(3), 1188–1202. https://doi.org/10.1017/S0954579421001115.

Dababnah, S., Shaia, W. E., Campion, K., & Nichols, H. M. (2018). "We had to keep pushing": Caregivers' perspectives on autism screening and referral practices of black children in primary care. *Intellectual and Developmental Disabilities, 56*(5), 321–336. https://doi.org/10.1352/1934-9556-56.5.321

Daftary, A. M. H. (2018). Critical race theory: An effective framework for social work research. *Journal of Ethnic & Cultural Diversity in Social Work,* 1–16. https://doi.org/10.1080/15313204.2018.1534223

Driscoll, K., Schonberg, M., Stark, M. F., Carter, A. S., & Hirshfeld-Becker, D. (2020). Family-centered cognitive behavioral therapy for anxiety in very young children with autism spectrum disorder. *Journal of Autism & Developmental Disorders, 50*(11), 3905–3920. https://doi.org/10.1080/15313204.2018.1534223

Early, B. P., & Grady, M. D. (2017). Embracing the contribution of both behavioral and cognitive theories to cognitive behavioral therapy: Maximizing the richness. *Clinical Social Work Journal, 45*(1), 39–48. https://doi.org/10.1007/s10615-016-0590-5

Eyler, J. R. (2018). *How humans learn: The science and stories behind effective college teaching.* West Virginia Press.

Freeman N. C., & Grigoriadis A. (2023). A survey of assessment practices among health professionals diagnosing females with autism. *Research in Developmental Disabilities, 135*, 104445. https://doi.org/10.1016/j.ridd.2023

Fuselier, M. N., Guzick, A. G., Bakhshaie, J., Wood, J. J., Kendall, P. C., Kerns, C. M., Small, B. J., Goodman, W. K., & Storch, E. A. (2023). Examining the relationship between anxiety severity and autism-related challenges during cognitive behavioral therapy for children with autism. *Journal of Autism & Developmental Disorders, 54*(5), 1849–1856. https://doi.org/10.1007/s10803-023-05912-z

Gannon, K. M. (2020). *Radical hope: A teaching manifesto.* West Virginia Press.

Gernsbacher, M. A. (2006). Toward a behavior of reciprocity. *Journal of Developmental Processes, 1*(1), 139–152. https://www.ncbi.nlm.nih.gov/pmc/articles/PMC4296736/

Gibson, A., Bowen, K., & Hanson, D. (2021). We need to talk about how we talk about disability: A critical quasi-systematic review. *In the Library with the Lead Pipe*, N.PAG. https://www.inthelibrarywiththeleadpipe.org/2021/disability/

Greene, R. W. (2010). *The explosive child: A new approach for understanding and parenting easily frustrated, chronically inflexible children.* HarperCollins.

Guzick, A. G., Schneider, S. C., Kendall, P. C., Wood, J. J., Kerns, C. M., Small, B. J., Park, Y. E., Cepeda, S. L., & Storch, E. A. (2022). Change during cognitive and exposure phases of cognitive–behavioral therapy for autistic youth with anxiety disorders. *Journal of Consulting and Clinical Psychology, 90*(9), 709–714. https://doi.org/10.1037/ccp0000755

Hartman, D., O'Donnell-Killen, T., Doyle, J. K., Kavanagh, M., Day, A., & Azevedo, J. (2023). *The adult autism assessment handbook.* Jessica Kingsly Publishers.

Hollocks, M. J., Wood, J. J., Storch, E. A., Cho, A., Kerns, C. M., & Kendall, P. C. (2022). Reward sensitivity predicts the response to cognitive behavioral therapy for children with autism and anxiety. *Journal of Clinical Child & Adolescent Psychology.* https://doi.org/10.1080/15374416.2022.2025596

Jones, K., Chapman, A., Edwards, P., & Cook, M. (2022). Evaluation of an adapted form of CBT for young people with a diagnosis of autism spectrum disorder (ASD) and anxiety. *Clinical Psychology Forum, 359*, 29–34. https://doi.org/10.53841/bpscpf.2022.1.359.29

Kamimura-Nishimura, K., Bush, H., de Lopez, P. A., Crosby, L., Jacquez, F., Modi, A. C., & Froehlich, T. E. (2023). Understanding barriers and facilitators of attention-deficit/hyperactivity disorder treatment initiation and adherence in Black and Latinx children. *Academic Pediatrics, 23*(6), 1175–1186. https://doi.org/10.1016/j.acap.2023.03.014

Katzman, M. A., Bilkey, T. S., Chokka, P. R., Fallu, A., & Klassen, L. J. (2017). Adult ADHD and comorbid disorders: Clinical implications of a dimensional approach. *BMC Psychiatry, 17*(1), 302. https://doi.org/10.1186/s12888–017 1463–3

Kilburn, T. R., Sørensen, M. J., Thastum, M., Rapee, R. M., Rask, C. U., Arendt, K. B., Carlsen, A. H., & Thomsen, P. H. (2023). Group based cognitive behavioural therapy for anxiety in children with autism spectrum disorder: A randomised controlled trial in a general child psychiatric hospital setting. *Journal of Autism and Developmental Disorders*, *53*(2), 525–538. https://doi.org/10.1007/s10803-020-04471-x

Lai, M. C., Kassee, C., Besney, R., Bonato, S., Hull, L., Mandy, W., Szatmari, P., & Ameis, S. H. (2019). Prevalence of co-occurring mental health diagnoses in the autism population: A systematic review and meta-analysis. *Lancet Psychiatry*, *6*(10), 819–829. https://doi.org/10.1016/S2215-0366(19)30289-5.

Lake, J., Modica, P. T., Chan, V., & Weiss, J. A. (2020). Systematic review comparing efficacy and effectiveness trials of cognitive behavioural therapy among youth with autism. *Autism*, 1–17. https://doi.org/10.1177/1362361320918751. https://pubmed.ncbi.nlm.nih.gov/32423224/

Lineberry, S., Bogenschutz, M., Broda, M., Dinora, P., Prohn, S., & West, A. (2023). Co-occurring mental illness and behavioral support needs in adults with intellectual and developmental disabilities. *Community Mental Health Journal*, *59*(6), 1119–1128 https://www.ncbi.nlm.nih.gov/pmc/articles/PMC9899157/

Mackelprang, R., Salsgiver, R., & Parrey, R. (2021). *Disability: A diversity model approach in human service practice* (4th ed.). Oxford University Press.

Mandell, D., Ittenbach, R., Levy, S., & Pinto-Martin, J. (2007). Disparities in diagnoses received prior to a diagnosis of autism spectrum disorder. *Journal of Autism & Developmental Disorders*, *37*(9), 1795–1802. https://doi.org/10.1007/s10803-006-0314-8

Mazefsky, C. A., & White, S. W. (2014). Emotion regulation: Concepts & practice in autism spectrum disorder. *Child Adolescent Psychiatry Clinics of North America*, *23*(1), 15–24. https://doi.org/10.1016/j.chc.2013.07.002

McBride, N. M., Weinzimmer, S. A., La Buissonnière-Ariza, V., Schneider, S. C., Ehrenreich May, J., Lewin, A. B., McGuire, J. F., Goodman, W. K., Wood, J. J., & Storch, E. A. (2020). The impact of comorbidity on cognitive-behavioral therapy response in youth with anxiety and autism spectrum disorder. *Child Psychiatry & Human Development*, *51*(4), 625–635. https://doi.org/10.1007/s10578-020-00961-2

Meyer, J., Ramklint, M., Hallerbäck, M. U., Lööf, M., & Isaksson, J. (2022). Evaluation of a structured skills training group for adolescents with attention-deficit/hyperactivity disorder: A randomized controlled trial. *European Child Adolescent Psychiatry*, *31*, 1–13. https://doi.org/10.1007/s00787-021-01753-2

Miller, H. L., Thomi, M., Patterson, R. M., & Nandy, K. (2023). Effects of intersectionality along the pathway to diagnosis for autistic children with and without co-occurring attention deficit hyperactivity disorder in a nationally-representative sample. *Journal of Autism & Developmental Disorders*, *53*(9), 3542–3557. https://doi.org/10.1007/s10803-022-05680-2

National Association for the Dually Diagnosed. (n.d.). *What is an IDD/MI dual diagnosis?* https://thenadd.org/idd-mi-diagnosis/

Norcross, J. C., & Lambert, M. J. (2018). Psychotherapy relationships that work III. *Psychotherapy*, *55*(4), 303–315. https://doi.org/10.1037/pst0000193

Pauli-Pott, U., Mann, C., & Becker, K. (2021). Do cognitive interventions for preschoolers improve executive functions and reduce ADHD and externalizing symptoms? A meta-analysis of randomized controlled trials. *European Child Adolescent Psychiatry*, *30*, 1503–1521. https://doi.org/10.1007/s00787-020-01627-z

Payne, M. (2020). *Modern social work theory* (5th ed.). Oxford University Press.

Pearson, A., Rose, K., & Rees, J. (2023). "I felt like I deserved it because I was autistic": Understanding the impact of interpersonal victimization in the lives of autistic people. *Autism: The International Journal of Research & Practice*, 27(2), 500–511. https://doi.org/10.1177/13623613221104546

Penot, J. (2024). *The unmasking workbook for autistic adults: Neurodiversity-affirming skills to help you live authentically, avoid burnout, and thrive.* New Harbinger Publications, Inc.

Perihan, C., Burke, M., Bowman-Perrott, L., Bicer, A., Gallup, J., Thompson, J., & Sallese, M. (2020). Effects of cognitive behavioral therapy for reducing anxiety in children with high functioning ASD: A systematic review and meta-analysis. *Journal of Autism & Developmental Disorders*, 50(6), 1958–1972. https://doi.org/10.1007/s10803-019-03949-7

Pickard, K., Blakeley-Smith, A., Boles, R., Duncan, A., Keefer, A., O'Kelly, S., & Reaven, J. (2020). Examining the sustained use of a cognitive behavioral therapy program for youth with autism spectrum disorder and co-occurring anxiety. *Research in Autism Spectrum Disorders*, 73.

Price, D. (2022). *Unmasking autism: Discovering the new faces of neurodiversity.* Harmony Books.

Ramirez, A. C., Grebe, S. C., McNeel, M. M., Limon, D. L., Schneider, S. C., Berry, L. N., Goin-Kochel, R. P., Cepeda, S. L., Voigt, R. G., Salloum, A., & Storch, E. A. (2020). Parent-led, stepped-care cognitive-behavioral therapy for youth with autism and co-occurring anxiety: Study rationale and method. *Brazilian Journal of Psychiatry / Revista Brasileira de Psiquiatria*, 42(6), 638–645. https://doi.org/10.1590/1516-4446-2020-0897

Robe, A., & Dobrean, A. (2023). The effectiveness of a single session of mindfulness-based cognitive training on cardiac vagal control and core symptoms in children and adolescents with attention-deficit/hyperactivity disorder (ADHD): A preliminary randomized controlled trial. *European Child Adolescent Psychiatry*, 32, 1863–1872. https://doi.org/10.1007/s00787-022-02005-7

Sauter, F. M., van den Bogaard, M., van Vliet, C., & Liber, J. M. (2023). An AAIDD-informed framework for cognitive behavioral case formulation and cognitive behavior therapy for young people with mild intellectual disabilities or borderline intellectual functioning. *Clinical Psychology: Science and Practice*, 30(3), 299–311. https://doi.org/10.1037/cps0000151

Sharma, S., Hucker, A., Matthews, T., Grohmann, D., & Laws, K. R. (2021). Cognitive behavioural therapy for anxiety in children and young people on the autism spectrum: A systematic review and meta-analysis. *BMC Psychology*, 9, 151. https://doi.org/10.1186/s40359-021-00658-8

Siegel, D. J., & Payne Bryson, T. (2011). *The whole-brain child: 12 revolutionary strategies to nurture your child's developing mind.* Bantam Books.

Silberman, S. (2015). *Neurotribes: The legacy of autism and the future of neurodiversity.* Penguin Random House.

Solish, A., Klemencic, N., Ritzema, A., Nolan, V., Pilkington, M., Anagnostou, E., & Brian, J. (2020). Effectiveness of a modified group cognitive behavioral therapy program for anxiety in children with ASD delivered in a community context. *Molecular Autism*, 11(1), 1–11. https://molecularautism.biomedcentral.com/articles/10.1186/s13229-020-00341-6

Storch, E. A., Wood, J. J., Guzick, A. G., Small, B. J., Kerns, C. M., Ordaz, D. L., Schneider, S. C., & Kendall, P. C. (2022). Moderators of response to personalized and standard care cognitive-behavioral therapy for youth with autism spectrum disorder and comorbid anxiety. *Journal of Autism and Developmental Disorders*, 52(2), 950–958. https://doi.org/10.1007/s10803-021-05000-0

Sze, K. M., & Wood, J. J. (2008). Enhancing CBT for the treatment of autism spectrum disorders and concurrent anxiety. *British Association for the Behavioural and Cognitive Psychotherapies, 36*(4). https://doi.org/10.1017/ S1352465808004384

Wang, X., Zhao, J., Huang, S., Chen, S., Zhou, T., Li, Q., Luo, X., & Hao, Y. (2021). Cognitive behavioral therapy for autism spectrum disorders: A systematic review. *Pediatrics, 147*(5), e2020049880. https://doi.org/10.1542/peds.2020–049880

Weir, E., Allison, C., & Baron-Cohen, S. (2021). The sexual health, orientation, and activity of autistic adolescents and adults. *Autism Research, 14*(11), 2342–2354. https://doi.org/10.1002/aur.2706

Wood, J. J., Kendall, P. C., Wood, K. S., Kerns, K. M., Seltzer, M., Small, B. J., Lewin, A. B., & Storch, E. A. (2020). Cognitive behavioral treatments for anxiety in children with autism spectrum disorder: A randomized clinical trial. *JAMA Psychiatry, 77*(5), 474–483. https://doi.org/10.1001/jamapsychiatry.2019.4160

Young, S., Adamo, N., Björk Ásgeirsdóttir, B., Branney, P., Beckett, M., Colley, W., Cubbin, S., Deeley, Q., Farrag, E., Gudjonsson, G., Hill, P., Hollingdale, J., Kilic, O., Lloyd, T., Mason, P., Paliokosta, E., Perecherla, S., Sedgwick, J., Skirrow, C., . . . Woodhouse, E. (2020). Females with ADHD: An expert consensus statement taking a lifespan approach providing guidance for the identification and treatment of attention-deficit/hyperactivity disorder in girls and women. *BMC Psychiatry, 20*(1), 1–27. https://eds.p.ebscohost.com/eds/pdfviewer/pdfviewer?v id=19&sid=a436f90f-afa0–424a-91a7–46bcebd45957%40redis

Emotion Chart (Optional)

Session 1

Six-year-old Emily walks into the therapy office, standing in her mother's personal space in a way that would typically be consistent of a younger child. Because she is following her mother so closely, it's not immediately apparent that she is rubbing her hands back and forth on her dress, likely stimming in order to help limit her anxiety being in a new place. Emily is very quiet, staring down at her feet. When she enters the room, she circles around a few times, looking at, but not touching, all of the items in the room. The therapist notes that Emily is avoiding the area where she is sitting, almost as if an invisible line is drawn on the floor. When the therapist asks if Emily would like to sit on the comfortable couch, Emily shakes her head and points to a small wiggle chair in the corner. The therapist smiles and nods that this is alright. Once Emily is seated, the therapist greets her and points to the, "How am I Feeling Today?" poster on the wall.

"Emily, do you want to make a chart like this one, but one where you get to choose the pictures?" the therapist asks.

Emily nods without speaking. The therapist continues, "I think it would be fun to make something special for you. Do you have a favorite show, game, or animal? We can make poster like this, but one that has your favorite thing."

Emily looks toward the therapist with interest and quietly says, "I love kitties!" and points to a small embroidered kitten on her dress, the very place where she had been rubbing her hands back and forth earlier when she was stressed.

The therapist nods her head, as it's obvious now she wasn't just rubbing the kitten but petting it. "That is perfect!" replies the therapist. "Let's make a kitty feelings chart." The therapist brings Emily to a chair next to her computer, opens up a web browser, and starts looking for pictures of kittens that fit each of eight emotions. As this activity continues, Emily goes from being shy and apprehensive, to laughing and fully engaging with the

DOI: 10.4324/9781003617181-2

therapist. Once the pictures are chosen, the therapist prints out two copies of the feelings chart, one to keep just like it is, and one to write on. Now that Emily has had time to transition, she is ready to talk about her own emotions.

Session Objectives

- Begin to establish rapport
- Introduce concept and communication of emotions
- Assess for knowledge and insight related to emotions and triggers

Emotion Chart (Optional)

This first step is recommended for younger children who are in kindergarten and first grade, or about ages 5 through 7. Most children are fairly comfortable with emotions after this age range. Use clinical judgment to decide if this session is appropriate for a client. The goal of this step is to set the stage and start having conversations about emotions. This conversation will not start with talking about the child's emotions, but rather about emotions as they relate to a favorite subject or special interest. This helps to start difficult conversations about emotions in a more neutral manner, and also helps to establish rapport. Many children are uncomfortable talking about their emotions, as they have often been made to feel shame about their feelings and the resulting behaviors. Establishing a trusting relationship is one of the most important factors in the success of any therapy interventions, so taking time to build rapport is just as important, if not more so, at this stage, as the tool itself (Norcross & Lambert, 2018).

Step 1

Explain to the parent that you want them in the session so that they can fully hear the explanations of the therapy tools, but that unless their child gets stuck and needs some prompting, you will be focused on the child and mostly ignoring them. Turn your focus to the child and ask if they have ever seen a feelings chart. Have an example of one for them to look at, then ask if they would like to make their own chart where they get to choose the theme and pictures. It is a good idea to set boundaries at this stage about the use of the computer in your office, such as whether or not they should touch the keyboard or mouse. Then, have the child sit beside you so that they can see the screen. After they have chosen a theme, use a search engine to choose images that show visuals of the following emotions: happy, mad, sad, worried, excited, frustrated, bored, and embarrassed. It is alright to be flexible with the emotions that are used, but it is recommended to use

Table 1.1 Color-coded text key

Happy	Green
Mad	Red
Sad	Blue
Worried	Yellow
Frustrated	Light red or orange
Excited	Light green
Bored	Gray
Embarrassed	Pink

at least the first five emotions. At this stage, do not discuss the child's emotions, but only the emotions of the characters or theme they have chosen. It is important for the child to choose the images independently and that the focus should be on what makes sense to the child, not what makes sense to the adults in the room. Let the child take the lead. It is possible to do this activity even if you have no knowledge of the chosen topic, such as a movie or show you have not seen. The only time a picture should be rejected is if the parent identifies it as being inappropriate.

Create an emotion chart using the template in Appendix A, or a word processing or design software of your choice. Be sure to use a landscape orientation so you have room to fit all the emotions and images on a single page. Crop the images as needed to focus on the characters or theme. Be sure that they all fit on the page and are a similar size. Color code the text to fit the emotions using Table 1.1. If you change some of the emotions, use your best judgment to match an appropriate color.

Step 2

Print out two copies of the chart, one for the child to keep just like it is, and one to write on. Hand them the one they get to keep, then sit with the child and ask them to identify at least two triggers that make them feel each of the eight emotions. Do not ask "if" they feel an emotion, but "when." For example, "When do you feel happy?," "When do you feel mad?," etc. Make sure that you use different colored markers or pens to match the color-coded font. This helps visual processors to take in the information. Try to use the child's exact wording, which demonstrates that you are listening. Writing out the answers also slows the activity, which gives the child additional time to process the information. If the child does not read, you can try drawing pictures, or letting them draw pictures. If you prefer, you can also type out the answers given on the chart before printing, just make sure that the answers are color coded to match the emotion.

One of the purposes of this activity is to gather information about how comfortable the child is with their emotions and how much self-insight they have. Try to have the child answer these questions independently, but if they are struggling, invite the parent to help prompt the child or give ideas. It may also be helpful for you to use mindful self-disclosure of what makes you feel each emotion to normalize the idea of having various emotions. Remember that many neurodivergent children have been shamed for their struggles with emotional regulation and anxiety, so knowing that you struggle too can help remove that shame. Invite parents to share their own emotion triggers for the same reason. Once the chart is done with at least two triggers for each emotion, spend the remainder of the session in a play activity to help continue to build a relationship with the child. Include the parent in the play activity as well. See herein for additional activities that you can do with the child if you find that their emotional insight is limited and that they need more time to learn about themselves, or what different emotions mean.

Figure 2.1 includes eight emotions, color coded, with a cat face to match. The chart also includes triggers for each emotion. The chart has two rows with four emotions each. Each emotion is listed in a specific color, with a corresponding cat face expressing the emotion listed, along with at least two triggers for each emotion. From top row, left

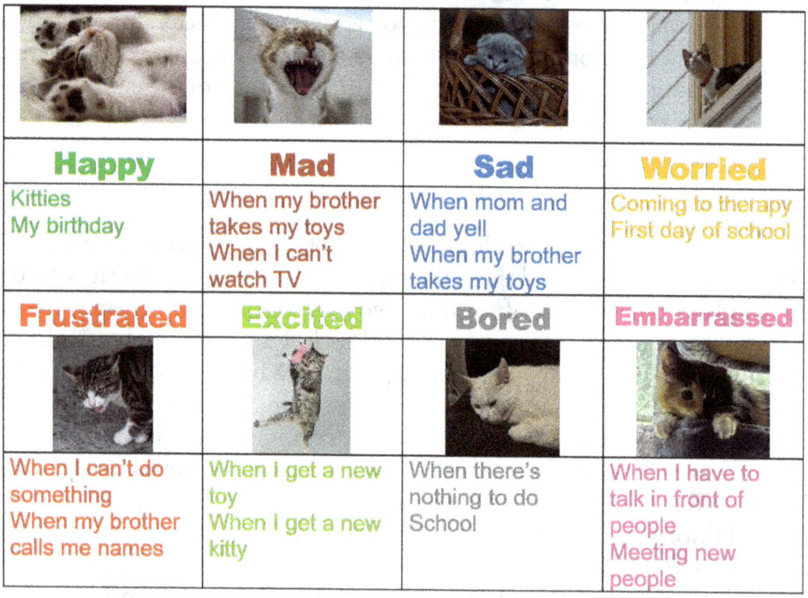

Happy	Mad	Sad	Worried
Kitties My birthday	When my brother takes my toys When I can't watch TV	When mom and dad yell When my brother takes my toys	Coming to therapy First day of school
Frustrated	Excited	Bored	Embarrassed
When I can't do something When my brother calls me names	When I get a new toy When I get a new kitty	When there's nothing to do School	When I have to talk in front of people Meeting new people

Figure 2.1 Emotion chart. Chart created by the author.

to right: happy-green. Triggers: kitties, my birthday. Mad-red. Triggers: when my brother takes my toys, when I can't watch TV. Sad-blue. Triggers: when mom and dad yell, when my brother takes my toys. Worried-yellow. Triggers: coming to therapy, first day of school. Second row: frustrated-orange. Triggers: when I can't do something, when my brother calls me names. Excited-light green. Triggers: when I get a new toy, when I get a new kitty. Bored-gray. Triggers: when there's nothing to do, school. Embarrassed-pink. Triggers: when I have to talk in front of people, when I meet new people.

Step 3

At the very end of session, talk to both the child and their parent and explain that their homework for the week is to practice using the emotion chart. Ask them to choose a place in their house where they can hang up the chart and see it on a regular basis. Talk about confidentiality and make sure that the child will not mind others in the family seeing the chart. If they do mind, they should choose a private location, like their room. Encourage both the child and parents to identify their emotions when they are feeling them throughout the next week. Remind parents that if their child is very mad, sad, or worried, they should either ask their child questions like, "Are you feeling mad?" or wait until later when the child is calm to talk about the emotions, rather than in the moment. Pointing to the images on the chart, rather than speaking, counts as communication. Explain to parents that research has shown that if you can help someone name their emotions, it helps to calm their brain and work toward self-regulation (Siegel & Payne Bryson, 2011).

Modification for Telehealth

This session can easily be done via telehealth. Instead of having the child sit beside you at the computer, use the screen share feature. Children may need help from parents on communicating to you what pictures they have chosen. Ask what row the picture is in and what number it is from the left. You can switch screen share from the web browser to the document screen, but it is also okay to leave the share feature on the web browser. Most children enjoy seeing the pictures of their favorite characters while they wait. When the child has chosen the final image for all eight emotions and you have added them to the chart, switch the screen share to the emotion chart and then ask what they think. After this, add the two triggers for each emotion as described earlier. If the parents have a color printer, then share via the telehealth platform or HIPAA-compliant email. If the family does not have a color printer, ask permission to mail the chart to the child.

Another option can be for the family to take a screen shot on the child's phone, tablet, or other device.

Co-parents and Multiple Caregivers

For children with caregivers who do not live together, it is important to ensure that the caregivers in these multiple households are familiar with the emotion chart. They should also be given information of how to support the use of this tool in the child's natural environment. This can be done through caregiver sessions, brief phone calls, or even secure emails. In these situations, you should print out multiple copies of the chart so that the child has one for each household.

Limited Insight

If the child presents with limited insight into their emotions, it is appropriate to spend a couple of weeks focused on this before moving on to the next session. Use play therapy games that focus on emotions. For example, choose a phrase like, "My favorite color is blue," but say it as if you were happy, mad, sad, etc. Another game is to roll a ball back and forth as if you were happy, mad, sad, etc. It also may be appropriate for you to use age-appropriate, mindful self-disclosure to identify your own emotions, encouraging parents to do the same. Often, children feel like they should not feel more negative emotions like sad or mad and this will help normalize them. Emotions are not good or bad, they are just how we feel.

Fatigue and/or Refusal

If you notice that the child has begun to struggle with maintaining attention, break the activity into parts, giving the child breaks to engage in other activities, or even wait to finish the activity until the next session. Remember that the relationship is more important than the tool, so focus on building rapport first. The same is true if the child refuses to engage in the activity. Children should be allowed to say no and forcing compliance only teaches children that they must obey authority figures without question. Teaching children to obey without question or protest can have long-term negative outcomes. Research has shown that this focus on compliance leads to increased victimization and abuse for neurodivergent children and adults (Pearson et al., 2023). You should honor a child's refusal to engage in an activity, even if the refusal comes across as rude or aggressive to adults. This type of behavior, which is frequently perceived as rude and aggressive by adults, often stems from the child's anxiety and is a stress response. When the child learns that they can trust the adult and that the adult is willing to listen to them, their stress levels will go down. Keeping stress levels down during sessions is very important, as increased stress inhibits the learning process (Eyler, 2018), meaning that children will not be able to fully engage with the CBT concepts that you are teaching them.

References

B. V. (n.d.). *Russian blue kitten on brown woven basket.* Pexels. https://www.pexels.com/photo/russian-blue-kitten-on-brown-woven-basket-127027/

Clk, H. (n.d.). *Curious cat peeking out of Istanbul window.* Pexels. https://www.pexels.com/photo/curious-cat-peeking-out-of-istanbul-window-30462488/

Demir, D. A. (n.d.). *Close-up of a tabby cat hissing.* Pexels. https://www.pexels.com/photo/close-up-of-a-tabby-cat-hissing-18540620/

Eyler, J. R. (2018). *How humans learn: The science and stories behind effective college teaching.* West Virginia Press.

Furkan. (n.d.). *A portrait of a little cat in bed.* Pexels. https://www.pexels.com/photo/a-portrait-of-a-little-cat-in-bed-16978945/

Gratisography. (n.d.). *Two brown tabby cats.* Pexels. https://www.pexels.com/photo/jumping-cute-playing-animals-4602/

Norcross, J. C., & Lambert, M. J. (2018). Psychotherapy relationships that work III. *Psychotherapy, 55*(4), 303–315. https://doi.org/10.1037/pst0000193

Pearson, A., Rose, K., & Rees, J. (2023). "I felt like I deserved it because I was autistic": Understanding the impact of interpersonal victimization in the lives of autistic people. *Autism: The International Journal of Research & Practice, 27*(2), 500–511. https://doi.org/10.1177/13623613221104546

Pixaby. (n.d.). *Close-up photo of cute sleeping cat.* Pexels. https://www.pexels.com/photo/close-up-photo-of-cute-sleeping-cat-416160/

Siegel, D. J., & Payne Bryson, T. (2011). *The whole-brain child: 12 revolutionary strategies to nurture your child's developing mind.* Bantam Books.

Usanakornkul, P. (n.d.). *Close up cute cat having big yawn showing sharp teeth and tongue with mouth open wide.* Pexels. https://www.pexels.com/photo/close-up-cute-cat-having-big-yawn-showing-sharp-teeth-and-tongue-with-mouth-open-wide-16597606/

Anger Scale

Session 2

Eight-year-old James arrives at his first therapy session, his hands balled into fists, his shoulders slightly tensed up, but still greeting the therapist despite his obvious anxiety. James continues to have slightly tense body language that appears to be his natural way of holding himself while in public. During the intake the prior week, James identified that he was there to talk about his anger. However, when the therapist asked what he felt his anger looked like, he only said, "Sometimes I yell and throw things." In continued conversations, it became obvious that his definition of anger was a reflection of what others told him was anger, that he often missed the earlier clues that his anger was building, and that by the time he identified that he was angry, it was usually too late to engage in any self-regulation activities. In the intake, he had also enthusiastically discussed his love of dinosaurs when the therapist had noted his dinosaur t-shirt. In fact, it took a significant amount of effort on the therapist's part to redirect the conversation back to complete the intake. Throughout the rest of the intake, James would suddenly interrupt and say, "I just remembered one more thing" and would need to finish the fact. When the therapist asked if it could wait until the end, James displayed significant anxiety.

For this first therapy session, because James did not present as needing the emotion chart tool due to his age and ease of discussing emotions in the intake, the therapist asks if James wants to create a 5-point anger scale. The therapist explains that the scale will feature levels of anger from 1, being happy and calm, to 5, being the angriest he could possibly get, and that he can use dinosaurs to discuss each level. James is very enthusiastic about this and happy to be able to freely talk to an adult about his favorite subject. Showing enthusiasm about this project, the therapist brings James to sit in a chair next to the computer to begin. James eagerly identifies the dinosaur species that he feels best fit with each level, and gives in-depth backgrounds on why each of the dinosaurs is a good representation of that level of anger. This shows that while he may not be able to verbalize the levels of anger in

DOI: 10.4324/9781003617181-3

himself, he is able to understand the concepts as evidenced by his descriptions of his favorite subject. With prompting and encouragement, he is ready to transition from discussing dinosaurs, to discussing his own anger levels. Having the example of the species to start makes identifying his own anger levels easier.

Session Objectives

- Continue to build rapport
- Create an emotion Likert scale to build recognition of size of emotions
- Assess for knowledge related to emotions and intensity of emotions

5-Point Anger Scale

For most children, this will be their first therapy session as the previous session focuses on an activity for younger children, or those with limited knowledge and comfort discussing emotions. This session should focus not only on identifying emotions but also on gaining insight into how big the child's emotions are. For most children, you will be making a 5-point anger scale. The scale can be used for any emotion in the future, but, for this session where the scale is introduced, the focus will be on anger. This is because anger is a more concrete emotion, and difficulty managing anger is often the reason neurodivergent children are referred for mental health treatment. The only exception to this is if the child is coming to therapy because they are struggling with anxiety and there is little to no struggle with anger. In this case, you would create a 5-point anxiety scale. You will be using the template from *The Incredible 5 Point Scale* (Buron & Curtis, 2022). This is a good resource for creating a Likert scale, which is common in cognitive behavioral therapy, as it utilizes multiple ways to present information including numbers, colors, and position on the page.

It is important for you to emphasize the number levels as you explain the tool. Communicating emotions using the number scale helps the child and their family to convey this information in a quick and functional way. For example, the family can do brief check-ins by asking, "What number are you?" The child can also let their family know that they are struggling in a confidential manner when out in the community if they are overwhelmed by saying, "I'm a 4," and the family will know that the child needs support, as well as what kind of support should be given. This is also useful in therapy where you can ask questions at the beginning of sessions like, "What was your highest number on your anger scale last week?" The child can name the number, and you will know what kind of week they had. In each of these examples, the goal is for the child to explain what is going on with their emotions without having to have extensive conversations about them. This makes communication about emotions easier and more accessible in times of high emotions.

Step 1

If this is the child's second session because they are younger and started with the emotion chart, start out by asking them to give an example of when they felt each of the eight emotions on their emotion chart. It is a good idea for you to give your own appropriate examples, and invite parents to do the same, in order to continue normalizing emotions. Next, explain to, or remind, the parent that you want them in session so that they can fully hear the explanations of the therapy tools, but that unless their child gets stuck and needs some prompting, you will be focused on the child and mostly ignoring them.

Switch your focus to the child, and let them know that they will be working with you to create a 5-point anger scale (or anxiety scale) with pictures from a preferred subject. Bring up the template on the computer and have the child sit beside you. If this is the first session, set boundaries about using the computer in your office. Using a web browser, go to images, and encourage the child to choose pictures that fit each anger level. Create the scale using the template in Appendix A, or the word-processing or design software of your choice. Be sure to use a portrait orientation so you have room to fit the scale on a single page. Crop the images as needed to focus on the characters or theme. Be sure that they all fit on one page and are a similar size. Again, children should be given autonomy to choose pictures that make sense to them. This activity can be done with a subject that you are unfamiliar with. The important part of the activity is that the scale makes sense to the child. Do not talk about the child's anger initially, but only anger as it relates to the theme they have chosen.

Dialogue 1

Anger Scale

LEVEL 1 (GREEN)

The first level is 1, or happy and calm. What dinosaur [theme of the scale will vary per child] is the happiest?

LEVEL 2 (BLUE)

Level 2 is just a little bit mad. We will call it, "irritated." What dinosaur is level 2, irritated?

LEVEL 3 (YELLOW)

Level 3 is just plan mad. This is when your mad is solid, but you can still control your anger. What dinosaur is level 3, mad?

LEVEL 4 (ORANGE)

Level 4 is really mad. This is when the mad starts to be harder to control. You are able to control it a little, but not completely. What dinosaur is level 4, really mad?

LEVEL 5 (RED)

Level 5 is when you can no longer control the mad. We can call this level a lot of things like furious, explosion, meltdown, super-duper mad, or something like that. What would you like to call level 5? [Let child choose the word that they feel best describes their level 5]. Okay, what dinosaur is level 5, [insert chosen adjective here]?

Dialogue 2

Anxiety Scale

Note that "anxiety" may not be an age-appropriate word that the child is familiar with. In this case, it is alright to use whatever word they are more comfortable with such as "worry," or "stress."

LEVEL 1 (GREEN)

The first level is 1, or happy and calm. What dinosaur [theme of the scale will vary per child] is the happiest?

LEVEL 2 (BLUE)

Level 2 is just a little bit anxious. We will call it "nervous." What dinosaur is level 2, nervous?

LEVEL 3 (YELLOW)

Level 3 is just plan anxious. This is when your anxiety is solid, but you can still control the anxiety. What dinosaur is level 3, anxious?

LEVEL 4 (ORANGE)

Level 4 is really anxious. This is when the anxiety starts to be harder to control. You are able to control it a little, but not completely. What dinosaur is level 4, really anxious?

LEVEL 5 (RED)

Level 5 is when you can no longer control the anxiety. We can call this level a lot of things like panic attack, freak-out, meltdown, shut-down, super-duper anxious, or something like that. What would you like to call level 5? [Let the child choose the word that they feel best describes their level 5]. Okay, what dinosaur is level 5, [insert chosen adjective here]?

Step 2

Now that the child has identified pictures for levels 1–5 related to their special interest, print out the scale and use markers that are color coded to match each level according to the colors in *The Incredible 5-Point Scale* (Buron & Curtis, 2022). Starting at level 1, go back to the above dialogue and say, "Now, we are going to go over what makes you feel each level. What makes you level 1, happy and calm? What makes you level 2, irritated?" and so on. Have the child give at least two examples of what triggers each level. If they are struggling to identify triggers, keep in mind that this may be because of low insight, or it may be because they are embarrassed. See herein for how to respond if either of these is the case. As you review triggers, be sure to remain neutral and matter of fact about what makes the child angry. This should be a judgment-free activity. Also, the goal of this step is not to get an extensive list of triggers, but to list at least two so that the child has a basic definition of what is meant by each level. Also, if you prefer, you can type out the answers given on the chart before printing; just make sure that the answers are color coded to match each emotion level.

Step 3

Once the child has given at least two triggers for each anger or anxiety level, let them know that you will be going back to level 1 and talking about behavior associated with the levels. "Now we are going back down to level 1 and we are going to talk about what each level looks like. If I were to walk into a room, how would I know that you were at a level 1? What would your face look like, what would you sound like, what would your muscles feel like?" Let the child describe what a level 1 looks like for them. At level 1, which is when the child is calm and regulated, it is alright to be a little leading in the questions. Avoid this for levels 2–5, however. For level 1, you can say, "What would your face look like? Would you be smiling or frowning or something in between? What would your voice sound like? Would you be loud or quiet, in the middle, or all of them? What do your muscles feel like? Would you be relaxed or tense or something in the middle?"

Once you have information for level 1, move to level 2, using the previous level to get more information. "What is different for level 2? Are you still smiling?" As you move up the levels, ask nonleading questions that will help you fill in as much information as possible in the space provided on the chart. One thing to keep in mind is that physical aggression will almost always go in level 5, so if the child says that they hit at levels 3 and 4, let them know that this is probably when control is gone, which belongs to level 5. You will be assessing for insight, and if insight is limited or not present, this tool will help build it. You can ask for parent input if the child is struggling. Again, what may look like lack of insight may be embarrassment. See herein for how to respond and ensure that you are responding to the information without judgment. Once this activity is complete, switch to a play activity for all but the last ten minutes of the session.

Figure 3.1 includes a visual scale from green at the bottom to red at the top. There are five levels of anger, color coded, with a dinosaur species to match each level, triggers for each level, and symptoms of what each level looks like. Listed from the bottom up: level 1, green, happy/calm. Triggers: playing video games, playing card games, playing with my friends. Symptoms: normal/neutral face, walking around, quiet unless I'm with friends, relaxed. Level 2, blue, irritated. Triggers: when my brother takes my chair, when my charger is missing, when my brother interrupts me. Symptoms: muscles a little tense, normal/neutral face, quiet, walking away. Level 3: mad, yellow. Triggers: when our plans to go somewhere change, when my brother takes my stuff. Symptoms: small frown, slightly tense, complaining, want to punch something. Level 4: really mad, orange. Triggers: when my computer keeps crashing, when my brother tackles me and gives me a noogie, when my brother takes my stuff. Symptoms: bigger frown, more tense, yelling, walking around, really want to punch something, throwing things. Level 5: furious, red. Triggers: when I have to stop playing video games, when someone deletes my progress on a game, when my brother tells his friends to call me names. Symptoms: super mad face, super tense, yelling, screaming, crying, swearing, punching stuff/people, throwing things, breaking things, hitting self.

Step 4

Encourage the child and parents to hang the anger or anxiety scale next to their emotion chart. If this is the first session, discuss the best place to put the scale where the child feels comfortable and will be reminded of it often. Their homework for the next week is to practice using the anger scale. Parents should do check-ins periodically, but avoid asking their child's anger level if they are clearly at a 4 or 5. Levels 4 and 5 are when the child is struggling to control their anger, so having someone ask what their level

Rating		What triggers my anger?	What my anger looks like.
5 Furious		When I have to stop paying video games When someone deletes my progress on a game When my brother tells his friends to call me names	Super mad face Super tense Yelling, screaming, crying, swearing Punching stuff/people Throwing things Breaking things Hitting self
4 Really mad		When my computer keeps crashing When my brother tackles me and gives me a noogie When my brother takes my stuff	Bigger frown More tense Yelling Walking around Really want to punch something Throwing things
3 Mad		When our plans to go somewhere change When my brother takes my stuff	Small frown Slightly tense Complaining Want to punch something
2 Irritated		When my brother takes my chair When my charger is missing When my brother interrupts me	Muscles a little tense Normal/neutral face Quiet Walking away
1 Happy and Calm		Playing video games Playing card games Playing with my friends	Normal/neutral face Walking around Quiet unless I'm with friends Relaxed

Figure 3.1 5-Point anger scale. Scale created by the author.

is will likely escalate the anger. Levels 4 and 5 are also when stress is very high, which is when our bodies are moving into fight, flight, and freeze mode and cognition decreases (Eyler, 2018). In these instances, encourage the parent to wait until everyone has calmed down to talk about their child's anger levels. Remind parents that part of the goal of the tool is to build insight. Some children will underrate or overrate their anger. In either case, when everyone is calm, the caregiver and child can have a discussion about why the parent thinks that the child was at a different level than the child did. For example, Emily tends to overrate her anger, so the parent would explain that while she said she was at a 5, she did not hit or scream, so was probably closer to 3 or 4. James tends to underrate his anger, so when he said he was a 2, he threw something, so he was more than irritated and likely at a 4 or 5.

Urge parents to also use the scale to describe their own anger. Explain that children know their caregivers get angry, but may not fully understand what triggers their anger or what an adult's regulation processes looks like. This tool will help parents and children better understand each other. Use an example that will help emphasize this such as the following conversation between a parent and child, "When you interrupted me, I asked you to stop so I could explain and I was at a 2. I started to talk again, you interrupted again, and then I was at a 3. I asked you to stop talking so I could explain what was going on. You interrupted again and I got to a 4 and I started to yell. I shouldn't have yelled. I was having a hard time going down my scale because I was being interrupted over and over, and I had a hard time calming down." These types of conversations let kids know that adults struggle with self-regulation too. Often, the next time a parent asks the child to stop so they can explain, the child has a better understanding of why the parent is asking, and will stop. In addition to helping to increase understanding between parent and child, having the parent use the tools helps to model how to use them, makes sure that a common language is being used, and helps parents to build their own emotional regulation skills.

Modification for Telehealth

As with the previous session, the anger scale can be created using the screen share option. Once the scale is complete, share it on the therapy portal or via secure email. If the family does not have a color printer, print the document and mail it with the family's permission. Another option can be for the family to take a screen shot on the child's phone, tablet, or other device.

Co-parents and Multiple Caregivers

Again, for children with caregivers who do not live together, it is important to ensure that caregivers in these multiple households are familiar with the therapy tools. You should give all caregivers information about how to support the use of the tools in the child's natural environment through open communication with their child's therapist. When you print out the anger or anxiety scale, you should print out multiple copies for the child to bring to each household.

Limited Insight or Embarrassment

It can be hard to tell if the child has limited insight, or if they are not answering because they are embarrassed. In both cases, it is appropriate for the therapist to use mindful self-disclosure to share their own triggers for each level. Keep examples general and age appropriate, and encourage parents to give examples as well. Often, if the child is not giving answers because they are embarrassed, they will start to share once the concept of feeling anger is normalized. If the child continues to struggle, it may be appropriate to have parents prompt the child to complete the anger scale. In either case, children should never be forced to talk about something they are not ready to.

If the child presents with very limited insight into their anger or anxiety levels, it is appropriate to spend a couple of sessions focused on this before moving on to the next step. Again, use play therapy games that focus on emotion levels similar to those used for the emotion chart. Choose a phrase like, "My favorite color is blue," but say it as if you are at levels 1–5. Play the ball-rolling game and roll the ball back and forth as if you were levels 1–5.

Caregiver Shaming

On occasion, caregivers will struggle to be nonjudgmental when talking about their child's anger levels. Gently remind the caregiver that this is to be a nonjudgmental activity without undermining them as caregivers. If they continue to struggle, state that you are going to take a break from the activity and play a game. Schedule a parent session where you can speak more directly to the caregiver about the importance of being nonjudgmental about the child's struggles. If the caregiver cannot do this, it is appropriate to meet with the child without the caregiver present and have the caregiver come in at the end of session to review homework and how to use the tool.

Fatigue and/or Refusal

If you note that the child has begun to struggle with maintaining attention, break the activity into parts and give the child breaks to engage in other activities, just like in the prior session. It is also appropriate to wait to finish the activity until the next session. Again, the relationship is more important than the tool, so focus on building rapport first. The same is true if the child refuses to engage in the activity. Children should be allowed to say no and teaching the child autonomy helps to prevent victimization (Pearson et al., 2023; Price, 2022).

Modification for Teens

To modify this activity for teens, complete the scale as described earlier, but consider leaving out the pictures. For those in their early teens, around middle school age, you may give them the choice to do the scale with or without pictures. Some older teens may want this choice as well. Use clinical judgment to decide. Also, for teens, in most cases, you will not have parents or caregivers present. Instead, with the teen's permission, do check-ins at the end of session to ensure that caregivers understand the tools.

Modification If the Number Scale Does Not Work: Change Your Approach

For some individuals, the number scale may not make sense, so changing the way that you are asking questions or introducing the concept might be helpful. It is also important when explaining any tool in this curriculum, to consider top-down versus bottom-up processing. Neurotypical individuals tend to take in information using top-down processing, or using prior knowledge to take in the whole picture and have a good idea of how to engage with the information (American Psychological Association, 2018b; Price, 2022). Neurodivergent individuals, especially those with Autism, tend to take in information using bottom-up processing, or taking in each piece of information separately, then building a whole picture of the information by putting all of the information together (American Psychological Association, 2018a; Price, 2022). Because of this difference, it may take neurodivergent people longer to process and they may need assistance in putting all of the pieces of information together into a coherent whole. This may mean that information may need to be broken down into smaller pieces and shared one piece at a time. For example, instead of asking what makes the child reach each level, ask what triggers their anxiety and then help them place each trigger on the scale. If they put an item in multiple places, that is okay. For example, reading aloud might be a 3 some days, but is often a 4, put it in both places. The goal is not to make a perfect scale, but to include enough examples that ensure that the child or teen understands the concept and can utilize the tool in their natural environment.

Modification If the Number Scale Does Not Work: How Big Is My Mad?

For some younger children, children with an intellectual disability, or children with specific learning disabilities, the number scale may not make sense to them, even after changing approaches. In this case, rather than using a number scale, use a scale focused on different-sized objects. A scale with different-sized balls represented by circles is a good tool, as balls are a familiar object that comes in all sizes. Start with three levels, or two if this will be easier for the child. If using two sizes, start with the smallest and largest, adding in the medium size once the extremes are mastered. This tool is adapted from another source which is listed in the references (Young, n.d.). Again, this tool can be used for any emotion, but starting with anger makes sense, as this is a more concrete emotion. If the child does not struggle with anger, start with anxiety.

Session 2: Adapted Anger Scale

The therapist reviewed the steps for making an anger scale with Emily and it was clear that she was not catching on. The therapist changed approaches, even sharing some appropriate personal anger triggers in order to illustrate examples, but Emily was still confused. She started to get frustrated and embarrassed.

"You know what Emily?" the therapist asked, "this is kind of confusing. Let's try something else. What do you think about making an anger scale with different-sized balls. What is the biggest ball you can think of?"

At this point, Emily's mother interjected, "Emily doesn't really use the word anger. Can we use "mad," instead?

The therapist nodded and thanked Emily's mom for this information. "Of course! What about making a mad scale then? What is the biggest ball you can think of?"

"The exercise ball my mom uses sometimes." Emily said, perking up a little.

"Perfect! Have you ever had mad that was that big?" asked the therapist.

"Yeah. One day when my brother took my toy, my mad got as big as that, maybe bigger even!"

"What is the smallest ball you can think of?" asked the therapist.

"Um, maybe a marble?" said Emily, tentatively.

"Yeah, a marble works. What makes you just a little mad, like marble sized?" asked the therapist.

"When my brother calls me a mean name," said Emily. "It would make my mad bigger, except I usually call him a name back, so it stays small."

"Excellent example, let's make a new chart!"

Steps

Let the child choose a theme and then ask them to choose three different-sized balls, very small, medium, and very large. For example, a marble, a basketball, and an exercise ball. Choose a picture as you would for the anxiety scale (see reference photo) and choose at least one trigger for each size of anger. For this modification, you will minimize what is written on the scale to reduce clutter, which makes the tool confusing. Write only one trigger for each size and discuss symptoms of each anger level, but do not write it on the scale. If time allows and it is appropriate, you can make additional scales that are color coded according to the colors on the emotion chart. For this tool, use the templates in Appendix A, or use a presentation program like PowerPoint, as this type of program is easier to use for this purpose. Note that the word "anger" is replaced by the word "mad" in this example versus the template in Appendix A. It is important that the words chosen for the emotions match the child's vocabulary.

Three red circles in Figure 3.2 represent three levels of anger in progressive sizes from small to large. The name of a ball that represents the size of each level is listed, along with one trigger for each level, and one cat displaying the size of the emotion. Small anger, marble-sized, trigger: when

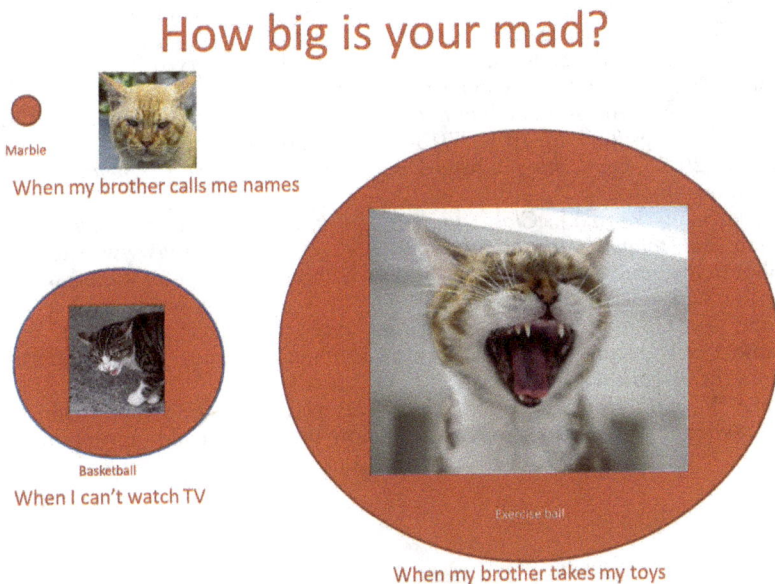

How big is your mad?

Marble

When my brother calls me names

Basketball
When I can't watch TV

Exercise ball

When my brother takes my toys

Figure 3.2 "How big is my mad?" scale created by the author.

my brother calls me names. Medium anger, basketball-sized, trigger: when I can't watch TV. Very big anger, exercise ball, trigger: when my brother takes my toys.

References

American Psychological Association. (2018a). *Bottom-up processing*. APA Dictionary of Psychology. https://dictionary.apa.org/bottom-up-processing

American Psychological Association. (2018b). *Top-down processing*. APA Dictionary of Psychology. https://dictionary.apa.org/top-down-processing

Bird, M. (n.d.). *Brown t-rex statue*. Pexels. https://www.pexels.com/photo/brown-t-rex-statue-410856/

Buron, K. D., & Curtis, M. (2022). *The incredible 5-point scale: Assisting students in understanding social interactions and controlling their emotional responses* (2nd ed.). 5 Point Scale Publishing.

Cup of Couple. (n.d.a). *Dinosaur toys on orange surface*. Pexels. https://www.pexels.com/photo/dinosaur-toys-on-orange-surface-8014524/

Cup of Couple. (n.d.b). *Triceratops dinosaur toys on a white surface*. Pexels. https://www.pexels.com/photo/triceratops-dinosaur-toys-on-a-white-surface-8014582/

Demir, D. A. (n.d.). *Close-up of a tabby cat hissing*. Pexels. https://www.pexels.com/photo/close-up-of-a-tabby-cat-hissing-18540620/

Eyler, J. R. (2018). *How humans learn: The science and stories behind effective college teaching*. West Virginia Press.

素材王国 Footage Kingdom. (n.d.). *Dinosaur on the ground*. Pexels. https://www.pexels.com/photo/dinosaur-on-the-ground-13825470/

Moto, K. (n.d.). *Portrait of an orange cat*. Pexels. https://www.pexels.com/photo/portrait-of-an-orange-cat-25881143/

Pearson, A., Rose, K., & Rees, J. (2023). "I felt like I deserved it because I was autistic": Understanding the impact of interpersonal victimization in the lives of autistic people. *Autism: The International Journal of Research & Practice*, 27(2), 500–511. https://doi.org/10.1177/13623613221104546

Price, D. (2022). *Unmasking autism: Discovering the new faces of neurodiversity*. Harmony Books.

Usanakornkul, P. (n.d.). *Close up cute cat having big yawn showing sharp teeth and tongue with mouth open wide*. Pexels. https://www.pexels.com/photo/close-up-cute-cat-having-big-yawn-showing-sharp-teeth-and-tongue-with-mouth-open-wide-16597606/

Wendt, L. G. (n.d.). *Dinosaur statue and dragon statue on a theme park*. Pexels. https://www.pexels.com/photo/dinosaur-statue-and-dragon-statue-on-a-theme-park-6489543/

Young, W. (n.d.) *How big is your child's anger?* Kidlutions: Solutions for Kids. https://kidlutions.blogspot.com/2012/05/how-big-is-your-childs-anger.html

Session 3

Stress Responses and Coping Skills List

Session 3

Emily happily bounds into session, smiling at the therapist, her mother trailing behind her. Emily immediately runs over to a small table and pulls out some crayons and a kitten coloring sheet. The therapist greets her enthusiastically and gives her a few minutes to transition to being in session. After the therapist can tell Emily is fully transitioned, the therapist asks how her last week has gone. After Emily describes her activities, the therapist asks, "What was your highest anger level this last week?"

Emily's smile fades a bit and she says, "4."

The therapist maintains a nonjudgmental tone and asked Emily what made her get to a 4. Emily responds that she got to a 4 when her brother took her toy. Emily spends a lot of time explaining why the toy is important and why she got so angry. She seems embarrassed, so the therapist responds by saying, "I got to a 4 too. Someone cut in front of me when I was driving and I yelled a word I shouldn't have. What did you do when you got to a 4?"

"I yelled too, and called my brother a mean name," Emily responds more comfortably.

"That happens when we get to a 4," the therapist adds, then works to transition to the session 3 activity, "Today, we are going to talk about our stress responses. But first, do you know what an instinct is?"

Session Objectives

- Continue to build and maintain rapport
- Introduce concept of stress responses and healthy coping skills
- Normalize stress responses
- Assess for knowledge related to stress responses

DOI: 10.4324/9781003617181-4

Stress Responses

Now that the child has built insight and communication skills related to their emotions, it is time to talk about how to respond to these emotions. To start, it is important to focus on stress responses. Our stress responses are instinctive reactions that humans have to emergency situations (Harvard Health Publishing, 2020). Neurodivergent children are often referred to therapy due to their anxiety and the subsequent stress responses they engage in, which are often seen as "problem behaviors." Because of this lack of understanding from adults, neurodivergent children often do not receive the support and understanding that they require, but instead are met with judgment, punishment, and shaming. This session is focused on the cognitive part of the CBT curriculum in which you as the therapist help reframe these behaviors so that the child and parent better understand and respond to the child's anxiety. It is important for you to emphasize that stress responses are instinctive and are therefore neither good nor bad. They are behaviors that are designed to keep us alive. While they evolved to be used in emergency situations, humans engage in them when they have big emotions as well. Stress responses reduce executive functioning like impulse control and emotional regulation. While these responses are neither good nor bad, they can be healthy and unhealthy. As a person goes up their anger or anxiety scale, it becomes harder to choose healthy stress responses (Eyler, 2018; Siegel & Payne Bryson, 2011). The work in therapy from here forward is supporting the child in finding healthy ways to engage in their stress responses when they are faced with big emotions. The focus is on giving the child permission to have stress responses, but in ways that ensure that they are not a danger to themselves or others. This will take time and repetition as the child works to create new habits.

When working on this step, it is important for children to learn healthy coping skills that fall into all three stress response categories: fight, flight, and freeze. Again, these responses are neither good nor bad, but often in mental health, we focus more on the flight and freeze responses through teaching mindfulness skills. For many individuals, especially for those who tend toward the flight and freeze responses, this is very effective. However, telling someone who is having an instinctive fight response to count to ten or engage in deep breathing is not going to be as effective as encouraging them to go for a walk or punch a punching bag. The fight response – and the anger that is the resulting emotion – is just as valid and just as likely to occur as the flight or freeze response.

At times, there is pushback on the concept of teaching healthy fight responses and concerns that giving kids an outlet for this response will lead to an increase in physically aggressive behaviors. The problem with this argument is that these kids are already engaging in physical aggression and this is often the reason they are being referred to mental health therapy. Kids and teens need ways to engage in their instinctive fight response safely in order to learn healthy regulation skills. Think of this through the lens of dialectical behavior therapy (DBT), where an individual and their therapist are identifying behaviors that the individual struggles to control, and helping the individual to identify more effective ways to engage in the behaviors (Payne, 2020). Also, think about the fact that there are many times that a fight response is very appropriate. For example, if a person were being attacked, fighting back may save their life. There should be no shame in any of our preprogramed instincts. They are neither good nor bad, but we need to learn healthy ways to engage in them.

Step 1

As in the example with Emily above, ask the child if they know what an instinct is. If they do not, explain that an instinct is something that our brains do automatically. Give a couple of examples like breathing or blinking to help explain the concept. Once the child understands the concept of an instinct, move to explaining stress responses as an instinct. The following dialogue outlines an example of this conversation.

Dialogue 3

Stress Responses

"Do you know what an instinct is?" the therapist inquires. Emily shakes her head without answering. "An instinct is something that our brains do automatically. We don't have to think about it, we just do it, like breathing. Do you have to think about breathing? Breathe in," the therapist breathes in an exaggerated fashion, "Breathe out," the therapist breathes out loudly.

"No!" Emily laughs.

"No!" the therapist replies. "What do your eyes do if something flies near them?"

"They blink!" shouts Emily

"That's right," agrees the therapist. "Our stress responses are things that we do in emergency situations that are designed to keep us alive. These stress responses are fight, flight, and freeze. Imagine you were walking down the street and you ran into a big, scary, mean dog. If you had a fight response, you would get ready to fight the dog and defend yourself. I don't recommend trying to fight a big, scary dog, but sometimes, you might have to in order to keep yourself safe." At this point in the dialogue, it would be beneficial for you to use a recent example from the media where someone was attacked by a large animal like a bear, cougar, or shark and survived because they engaged in a fight response. "If you have a flight response, which is a fancy word for runaway really fast, when that dog comes toward you, you turn around and run the other direction before you really even know what has happened. If you have a freeze response, your brain kind of shuts off. You can't really move, talk, or think. A lot of times, if an animal like a dog sees you having this kind of response, it will decide you aren't a threat and leave you alone."

"So, the thing about stress responses is that we don't just have them when we are in emergency situations," the therapist continues. "We also have them when we have really big emotions like when we are really mad, really sad, really scared, or really anxious. These are our level 4 and level 5 responses. When people have level 4 and level 5 emotions, their brain tells them to go into their fight, flight, or freeze mode. When people have big emotions and go into a fight response, they will yell, scream, stomp, hit things or people, slam doors, and look angry. When people go into a flight response, they will walk away in the middle of an argument, or hide from people or things that are stressing them out. Their brains are telling them to get as physically far away as they can from whatever caused their stress response. When they go into a freeze response, their brains tell them to get mentally far away from whatever caused their stress response. People in a freeze response will space out, or are always on their phones, watching TV, playing video games, or even reading. They want to turn their brain off and go to their happy place."

"Now we all do all three stress responses, but we usually have a 'favorite,' that we do most often. What do you think is your favorite stress response?"

Emily responds that she usually goes into a fight response. Her mother agrees. The therapist then shares her main or "favorite" stress response and invites Emily's mother to do the same. The purpose of this is to normalize the concept of having a stress response.

Step 2

The next step is to introduce the concept of healthy versus unhealthy stress responses. The following dialogue focuses on James as the therapist outlines this information. This dialogue uses a real example from my own childhood to explain the difference between a healthy and unhealthy fight response. Choose your own example in place of the one below. The reason for using mindful self-disclosure in this step is not only to normalize the experience of having a stress response but also to demonstrate that everyone struggles with self-regulation.

Dialogue 4

Stress Responses Continued

"Our stress responses are instincts that help keep us safe, but there are healthy and unhealthy ways to engage in our fight, flight, and freeze behaviors," the therapist explains. "I outlined some of the unhealthy behaviors before, but before I talk about healthy fight, flight, and freeze behaviors, I want to tell you a story. Remember, I said my favorite stress response is fight? When I was about 10 or 11 years old, my mom said that we were going to go to the neighbor's house. I got really excited because I loved my neighbor. She was like having an extra grandma just across the street. It was January and snowy outside, so I ran and got on my coat and snow boots. My mom looked in the kitchen and said that I couldn't come yet because the dishes were not done. I didn't think this was fair and got to a level 4 on my anger scale. When my mom and my brother left to go to the neighbors, I went into my brother's room where I could see them walk across the yard and I went up to a level 5. I meant to kick the wall, but I kicked the window instead. What do you think happened when I kicked the window with my snow boots on?"

"You broke it!" James shouts.

"Now, what do you think would happen if I got really mad at my paperwork when I was at my office, which definitely happens, and I got up and kicked out my window?"

"You would get fired," James responds.

"Would your mom or dad want you to work with a therapist who gets mad and kicks out windows?"

"No!" exclaims James while his dad shakes his head in agreement.

"So," continues the therapist, "when I get to a level 4 or 5 at the office because I am mad at my paperwork, I go tell the receptionist that I am going to go for a walk. I walk around the block a couple times, making sure that I get my heart rate up, and this helps me to calm down."

"Healthy fight responses can be things like walking, riding a bike, playing basketball, punching a punching bag, or other things that get my heart rate up or use my muscles, "the therapist continues. "A healthy flight response would be telling someone that you need a break and going to a quiet place to calm down. You have to make sure that once you are calm, you go back and deal with the problem that caused your stress response. For healthy freeze responses, there is nothing wrong with being on your phone, playing video games, watching TV, or reading, but it can become unhealthy if this is all you do. You do it for a little while until you are calm, then go back and deal with the thing that caused your stress response."

Step 3

After reviewing the information from step 2, explain that the next step is making a coping skills list. Open up a word processing document and write, "Coping Skills List" in the child's favorite color in large, bold font across the top in the center. Underneath, write in parentheses in a smaller font so that the text fits in one line, "(Things that make me feel happy and calm)." This helps to define "coping skills" for the child. On the next line, create bullet points, change the format to "align left," and ask, "What makes you feel happy and calm?" I encourage the child to come up with at least 10–12 items for their list, ensuring that they include healthy items from all three stress responses, especially the stress response that they engage in most often. Some children come up with their list easily, others struggle. Ask questions about activities they like including physical activities, shows, video games, art, music, play activities, time with pets, etc. Once they have about 10–12 items, invite them to choose a picture that makes them think happy and calm thoughts to put on the bottom, then print out the list. As with previous sessions, the rest of the session can be spent in a play activity.

In Figure 4.1, the text is from top down: Title: Coping skills list. Subtitle: things that make me happy and calm. Contains a photo of a happy

Coping Skills List

(Things that make me happy and calm)

- Playing video games
- Playing basketball
- Drawing pictures
- Watching a show
- Practicing karate
- Punching bag
- Snuggling with a blanket
- Petting the dog
- Petting the cat
- Legos
- Asking for a hug
-

Figure 4.1 Coping skills list. Created by the author.

dinosaur in the bottom right corner. Contains the following coping skills listed with bullet points: playing video games, playing basketball, drawing pictures, watching a show, practicing karate, punching bag, snuggling with a blanket, petting the dog, petting the cat, Legos, asking for a hug.

Step 4

During the last 5–10 minutes of session, outline the homework. Encourage the family to hang the coping skills list with the previous tools made in session. When the child starts to go up their anxiety scale, they should look at their coping skills list and find something that will help them go back down. Speaking directly to the child, remind them that they may not be able to do all of the items on the list all of the time. Joke that just because they put "play video games" on their coping skills list does not mean that they can play whenever they go up their anger scale. If the parent or caregiver says no, they need to choose something else. Remind parents to help the child match the coping skill to the stress response if possible.

Modification for Telehealth

All of the above can be done via telehealth with the screen-share option. As before, share the tool on the telehealth portal via secure email or traditional mail service.

Co-parents and Multiple Caregivers

Ensure that the child has this tool printed out for each household and that the caregivers understand how to support their child's use of the tools.

Struggles With Finding 10–12 Coping Skills

As noted earlier, some children may struggle to identify more than a couple of potential coping skills. If therapist and caregiver prompting has not increased the list sufficiently, this is a good indication that the child needs to spend time exploring new potential coping skills. It is recommended in this case to spend the next one to three sessions exploring healthy coping skills with a focus on the child's "favorite" stress response.

Fatigue and/or Refusal

Again, if the child has begun to struggle with attention, take a break. This session is structured with the therapist giving more psychoeducation than previous sessions. For many neurodivergent children, sitting through a lot of adult talking is very tiresome. Make sure to be animated and use drawings, toys to act out the dialogue, or other tools that will help increase the child's processing and help maintain their attention. If the child refuses to engage, end the activity and switch to a play activity to build rapport. Let them know at the end of session that you will try to finish the coping skills list next time.

Modification for Teens

This activity can be done as written earlier – ensuring that content, including psychoeducation, examples, and coping skills are age-appropriate.

References

Cup of Couple. (n.d.a). *Dinosaur toys on orange surface.* Pexels. https://www.pexels.com/photo/dinosaur-toys-on-orange-surface-8014524/

Eyler, J. R. (2018). *How humans learn: The science and stories behind effective college teaching.* West Virginia Press.

Harvard Health Publishing. (2020, July 6). *Understanding the stress response.* https://www.health.harvard.edu/staying-healthy/understanding-the-stress-response

Payne, M. (2020). *Modern social work theory* (5th ed.). Oxford University Press.

Siegel, D. J., & Payne Bryson, T. (2011). *The whole-brain child: 12 revolutionary strategies to nurture your child's developing mind.* Bantam Books.

Anger Switches

Session 4

James bursts into session and, completely unprompted, loudly states that he got to a 5 the previous week. The therapist, in a neutral tone, asks what got him to a level 5. James states that his sister took his dinosaur plushy and would not give it back. The therapist empathizes with this, by stating, "I'm sorry that happened. I can understand why you got to a 5. What happened then?"

"She didn't say she was sorry or anything, and then she made me get in trouble," shares James.

"How did she make you get in trouble?" the therapist asks.

"I screamed at her and chased her, and then hit her. It was her fault."

"You screamed, chased her, and hit your sister," the therapist states matter-of-factly, "Then what happened?"

"Well," continues James, "I was sent to my room. When I came out, Dad reminded me of my coping skills list. I was still a 3, so I picked, 'punch my punching bag,' and I hit that instead. That made me get to a 1 or 2."

"So, you got to a 5 and hit your sister, then you went to your room, remembered your coping skills list with Dad's help, and then used that to calm down the rest of the way. That's good James! We don't want you to hit your sister, that's an unhealthy fight response, but remember that you are practicing and learning. You'll remember faster next time!"

"I will!" James exclaims.

Session Objectives

- Continue to build and maintain rapport
- Apply and practice concepts

DOI: 10.4324/9781003617181-5

Anger Switches

This activity is a simple worksheet that ties previous concepts together. This activity is meant to be a brief review, as well as a transition from skill building to practice and repetition. The child is not expected to write out the answers, as writing is often an adverse activity for neurodiverse children. Instead, the therapist will write what the child says unless the child expresses the desire to do it themselves. When the worksheet is done, the remainder of session will be spent on play activities of the child's choosing.

Step 1

After a check-in like the one outlined earlier, print out a copy of the anger switches worksheet and make sure that you have red and green pens or markers to write with. This tool is adapted from another source which is listed in the references (Greenwald et al., 2008). Read through the text on the worksheet. "We all have things that switch our anger on and things that switch our anger off. We're going to call these: anger switches. On the left," point to the red rectangles on the left, "we are going to write down things that switch our anger on. On the right," point to the green rectangles, "we are going to write down things that switch our anger off." Then, point to the first "switch" as if you were pushing it and ask, "What is something that switches your anger on?" Write down what the child says in red. Then ask, "What could you do to switch your anger off?" Write down the response in green. Go down the line and do at least four examples. Note in the example below that the first item on the list is the one shared in James's story. This helps to reinforce concepts using a relevant and recent example.

In Figure 5.1, the text is arranged in two columns with red on the left representing things that turn anger "on," and green on the right representing things that turn anger "off." Text starting at the top: Everyone has things that switch their emotions on and off. Second line: What are things that switch your anger on, and what could you do to switch your anger off? Two rectangles are placed below text, red on the left with the word, "on" above it, green on the right with the word "off" above it. The next line of text: On the left, write down things that switch your anger on. On the right, write down things that could switch your anger off. Below the text are five red rectangles on the left and five green rectangles on the right. Examples are written to the left of the rectangles. On: When my sister broke my toy; off: Punch a punching bag. On: When I can't play video games; off: Play Legos. On: When I can't play with my friends; Off, Play with the dog. On: When Mom or Dad say no; Off: Find something else to do.

Everyone has things that switch their emotions on and off.

What are things that switch your anger on, and what could you do to switch your anger off?

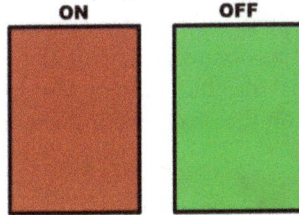

On the left, write down things that switch your anger **on**. On the right, write down things that could switch your anger **off**.

	ON		OFF
◼	When my sister broke my toy.	◼	Punch a punching bag.
◼	When I can't play video games.	◼	Play Legos.
◼	When I can't play with my friend.	◼	Play with the dog.
◼	When Mom or Dad say no.	◼	Find something else to do.
◼		◼	

Figure 5.1 Anger switches. Chart created by the author.

Anxiety Switches

For those individuals who do not struggle with anger, but do struggle with anxiety, complete the above, but use "anxiety" or "worry" in place of anger as well as the "Worry Switches" template, found in Appendix A.

Modification for Telehealth

This activity can be done via telehealth with the screen-share option. As before, share the tool on the portal, via secure email, or traditional mail service.

Co-parents and Multiple Caregivers

As this tool is mostly for reinforcement of previously learned skills, the child does not necessarily need a copy for each household, but you should continue to ensure that all caregivers are involved with care.

Fatigue and/or Refusal

This activity can be done briefly, but some children may still need breaks. If this occurs, alternate completing one line on the worksheet with a play activity, then the next line and a play activity, until you complete at least four lines. Again, the purpose of this activity is to transition from learning new skills and tools each session to practicing the skills. If the child refuses to do the worksheet, that is alright. It can be sent home for them to do with their caregivers, worked on the next session, or not completed at all.

Modification for Teens

This activity is optional for teens. Some teens will benefit from this type of review; others will find it unhelpful or even childish. Use clinician judgment, and if in doubt, show the teen the activity and ask if they want to complete it for review or not.

Reference

Greenwald, A. F., Pelta-Heller, Z., & Shapiro, L. E. (2008). *I'm not bad, I'm just mad: A workbook to help kids control their anger.* Instant Help Books.

Session 5

Caregiver Session

Session Objectives

- Check in with parents to interpret:
  - How they feel child is applying tools
  - Ways to increase application and generalization of tools in the child's natural environment
- Answer parents' questions
- Introduce and review additional concepts:
  - The 'fawn response'
  - Intersectionality

Caregiver Session

Every five weeks, you should check in with the parents or caregivers to gather information, answer questions, and problem-solve areas of continued need. For these sessions, it is best to not have the child present so that the parents can speak openly without the child feeling like they are being criticized. Since caregivers are the ones who will most likely be with the child in those moments when big emotions happen, they will need space to process and problem-solve the tools. Think of this as a coaching session where the therapist helps the caregiver to fine-tune strategies. The therapist is also working to gather more information about the child from the person or people who know the child best. In this session, ask the parent what is going well, what is not going well, and answer any questions that they may have about treatment thus far. Just as it is important to build trust and rapport with the child, you need to build trust with caregivers as well. After all, they are trusting you to care for their child. It is very important that while you may be an expert on content, the parent is the expert on the

DOI: 10.4324/9781003617181-6

child. The goal is to work together to brainstorm strategies that will work best for the individual child.

Co-parents and Multiple Caregivers

If possible, have all parents and caregivers meet at the same time to ensure that everyone gets the same information. If this is not possible due to differing schedules or co-parents who struggle to get along, separate sessions can be scheduled. Keep careful notes of what information you give each session and ensure that each caregiver receives the same basic information. Keeping careful session notes will help you ensure that the information shared in each caregiver session is consistent.

Fawn Response

In addition to a parent check-in, you will be covering one additional stress response: the fawn response. This is a relatively new concept in psychology, and it describes an instinctive response to appease another individual in order to avoid harm to self. Another way to describe this stress response is an overwhelming need to please others. This stress response is common not only in situations where there is abuse but also in marginalized populations, such as the neurodivergent community. This response is meant to avoid rejection, escape bullying, or to gain friends. The fawn response often occurs when a fight, flight, or freeze is not possible or will not lead to positive outcomes. It often becomes a person's primary stress response when they have repeatedly experienced poor outcomes after having had a fight, flight, or freeze response (Schlote, 2023).

The fawn response is common in neurodivergent children in part because the focus of many disability interventions has historically been, and continues to be, on teaching compliance (Silberman, 2015). Neurodivergent children are taught through these compliance-based interventions that their needs and desires are not as important as pleasing authority figures. This continues as neurodivergent children grow into adults and internalize ableist messages about themselves, leading to higher rates of victimization (Pearson et al., 2023; Price, 2022), being in abusive relationships, turning to substances, struggling with mental health, and other long-term, negative outcomes (Price, 2022).

Parents will likely be concerned upon hearing this information, so make sure to use active listening skills to allow them to process and answer any questions they may have. Make sure to also focus on good news: it is not too late to help their child manage the fawn response. As with any of the stress responses, the fawn response is not good or bad. Sometimes, it may be necessary to appease others. For example, if someone were to threaten you with a gun and demand your wallet, handing the wallet over, or appeasement, would be safer than trying to fight the person or run away. It is when an individual consistently ignores their own needs and interests in order to appease others that this response becomes a problem.

To help support a child who may rely too much on the fawn response, advise caregivers to allow their child to say no, to negotiate, and to encourage them to listen to their child. A great resource to help parents learn more about negotiating with their child is the book by Ross Greene (2010), *The Explosive Child*, which is available in both print and audio forms. Strategies in this book can be used with children who tend toward any of the stress responses, including fawning. It may take time for parents to get used to this approach and for the child to get used to self-advocating, but just like with any of the skills covered in this curriculum, it takes practice and repetition.

Coordination of Care

Children do better if all their support systems are using the same tools and language. During the caregiver session, discuss if caregivers feel it would be appropriate to share tools with the child's school, coaches, other service providers, or anyone else in their support system. You should also ask the child this question in the next session to ensure that they feel comfortable sharing the visuals they have made. It would be appropriate to work with the child to make modified tools that do not have confidential information. If possible, you should meet with the child's other support systems to help explain how to use the tools. If this is not possible, discuss with the parent and child how to teach others in their support system to use the tools.

In the example below, James was fine with his teacher seeing what his anger levels looked like. He reasoned that his teacher saw them at school, and already knew this information. He was uncomfortable with identifying his triggers, however, so he and his therapist decided to change this column, presented in Figure 6.1, to include the definition of the anger levels.

The chart includes a visual scale from green at the bottom to red at the top. There are 5 levels of anger, color coded, with a dinosaur species to match each level, triggers for each level, and symptoms of what each level looks like. Listed from the bottom up: level 1, green, happy/calm. Description: when I feel happy and calm. No anger. Symptoms: normal/neutral face, walking around, quiet unless I'm with friends, relaxed. Level 2, blue, irritated. Description: just a little anger. Frustrated. Symptoms: muscles a little tense, normal/neutral face, quiet, walking away. Level 3: mad, yellow. Description: just plain mad. Anger is solid, but I can control it. Symptoms: small frown, slightly tense, complaining, want to punch something. Level 4: really mad, orange. Description: my anger is bigger. I can kind of control it, but not very well. Symptoms: bigger frown, more tense, yelling, walking

Rating		What triggers my anger?	What my anger looks like.
5 Furious		My anger is too big to control. My anger is in control, I am not. I am in my fight response.	Super mad face Super tense Yelling, screaming, crying, swearing Punching stuff/people Throwing things Breaking things Hitting self
4 Really mad		My anger is bigger. I can kind of control it, but not very well.	Bigger frown More tense Yelling Walking around Really want to punch something Throwing things
3 Mad		Just plain mad. Anger is solid, but I can control it.	Small frown Slightly tense Complaining Want to punch something
2 Irritated		Just a little anger. Frustrated.	Muscles a little tense Normal/neutral face Quiet Walking away
1 Happy and Calm		When I feel happy and calm. No anger.	Normal/neutral face Walking around Quiet unless I'm with friends Relaxed

Figure 6.1 5-Point anger scale, revised for use in school. Scale created by the author.

around, really want to punch something, throwing things. Level 5: furious, red. Description: my anger is too big to control. My anger is in control, I am not. I am in my fight response. Symptoms: super mad face, super tense, yelling, screaming, crying, swearing, punching stuff/people, throwing things, breaking things, hitting self.

Modification for Teens

For some younger teens, scheduling the parent session without the teen is appropriate, but not for all. For most older teens, parental involvement will be less direct and the focus will be on the teen. As with all interventions, the clinician must consider the child or teen's chronological and developmental age. For teens who are able to be more independent, it would be appropriate to ask permission to meet with parents without them, explaining that the goal is not to discuss them without their permission, but to discuss the tools and go over some additional information that parents need to know to help them more effectively.

Intersectionality

In this parent session, it is recommended that the therapists review any issues of intersectionality that may create additional stressors for the child. Discuss with the parent what these potential stressors may be, as well as brainstorm ways to minimize these additional stressors. Give the parent any applicable resources, such as online or in-person support groups, information, or other potential resources. Review information about intersectionality in the introduction of this curriculum before meeting with parents.

References

Bird, M. (n.d.). *Brown t-rex statue*. Pexels. https://www.pexels.com/photo/brown-t-rex-statue-410856/

Cup of Couple. (n.d.a). *Dinosaur toys on orange surface*. Pexels. https://www.pexels.com/photo/dinosaur-toys-on-orange-surface-8014524/

Cup of Couple. (n.d.b). *Triceratops dinosaur toys on a white surface*. Pexels. https://www.pexels.com/photo/triceratops-dinosaur-toys-on-a-white-surface-8014582/

素材王国 Footage Kingdom. (n.d.). *Dinosaur on the ground*. Pexels. https://www.pexels.com/photo/dinosaur-on-the-ground-13825470/

Greene, R. W. (2010). *The explosive child: A new approach for understanding and parenting easily frustrated, chronically inflexible children*. HarperCollins.

Pearson, A., Rose, K., & Rees, J. (2023). "I felt like I deserved it because I was autistic": Understanding the impact of interpersonal victimization in the lives of autistic people. *Autism: The International Journal of Research & Practice*, 27(2), 500–511. https://doi.org/10.1177/13623613221104546

Price, D. (2022). *Unmasking autism: Discovering the new faces of neurodiversity*. Harmony Books.

Schlote, S. (2023). History of the term "appeasement": A response to Bailey et al. (2023). *European Journal of Psychotraumatology*, 14(2), 1–4. https://doi.org/10.1080/20008066.2023.2183005

Silberman, S. (2015). *Neurotribes: The legacy of autism and the future of neurodiversity*. Penguin Random House.

Wendt, L. G. (n.d.). *Dinosaur statue and dragon statue on a theme park*. Pexels. https://www.pexels.com/photo/dinosaur-statue-and-dragon-statue-on-a-theme-park-6489543/

Practice, Problem-Solve, and Perfecting Skills, Part 1

Sessions 6–9

Emily has been coming to therapy for just over a month. Her parents report that she is feeling more confident in communicating her emotions, and getting better at finding ways to manage those emotions. As more and more people in her life use the scale with her, she is not only able to generalize the skills to different people and locations but also relying on them less and reports lower anxiety about people understanding what she is trying to convey. Her parents are also feeling more confident in how to support Emily when she has big emotions. Her teachers have noted positive changes as well. She is more confident with peers and has started raising her hand to answer questions in class more often. The teacher also shared with her parents that when a peer took Emily's favorite pencil, she loudly asked for it back, but did not hit the peer, which is what she had done in the past. Some of her peers also have started talking to her about kittens and have begun playing a kitten game with her on the playground.

Session Objectives

- Continue to build and maintain rapport
- Practice, problem-solve, and perfect use of CBT tools

Practice, Problem-solve, and Perfecting Skills

The purpose of the remainder of individual sessions is to spend time practicing the tools. Activities should be tailored to the child and their interests. The goal is to be creative, make the activities relatable, problem-solve any areas of need, and continue to build and maintain rapport. At this point in therapy, it is less necessary for parents to be present through the whole

DOI: 10.4324/9781003617181-7

session, so use your clinical judgment to decide if you will continue meeting with the child and parent, or just the child. If you are meeting with just the child, it is still important to do a check-in with parents for 10–15 minutes either at the beginning or at the end of each session.

There are many potential ways to practice and reinforce skills, and which strategies you use will be dependent on the individual child. Keep in mind the child's strengths and needs. Follow the child's lead and let them choose activities. Make sure that you have options and variety available. Some children, especially autistic children, may prefer to do the same activities each week. Others, especially those with ADHD, will crave variety and novelty. With each session, make sure that you are doing a check-in to assess anger or anxiety levels from the previous week. This gives you and the child the opportunity to discuss and celebrate progress, as well as problem-solve areas of continued need. Ask the following questions as appropriate:

- What was your highest anger/anxiety level?
- How many times did you get to that level?
- What made you get to that level?
- What happened after you got to a 5 (or highest number)?
- What could you do next time instead of (insert unhealthy response here)?

The purpose of these check-ins should never be to pass judgment or express disappointment. The purpose is to measure progress, celebrate wins, and discuss how to continue to work on therapy goals. These discussions may also inform what activity should be done to practice and refine the CBT tools.

Explore New Coping Skills

An engaging activity is to give lists of healthy coping skills that fall into the fight, flight, and freeze categories and let the child pick what they want to practice. This activity is also helpful for children who have limited coping skills. Below are some examples. This is not an exhaustive list, so feel free to add additional strategies.

Fight

- Hit a playground ball against the wall
- Do jumping jacks

- Smash empty egg cartons
- Pop bubble wrap
- Punch a punching bag
- Dance
- Go for a walk or run

Flight

- Go to a quiet place
- Take a break from a stressful activity and come back later
- Exercise
- Take some time to be alone

Freeze

- Read
- Listen to or play music
- Deep breathing exercise
- Do yoga
- Play a video game
- Color/draw

Exercise

Exercise is a very important tool for managing anxiety. Physical activity that raises a person's heart rate causes the brain to release natural, anti-anxiety brain chemicals (Ratey, 2019; Sirotiak et al., 2023). It then turns on the prefrontal regions of the brain which control executive functions, and turns down the activity in the amygdala, which controls the instinctive parts of the brain, which leads to fight, flight, or freeze mode (Ratey, 2019; Schoenfeld et al., 2013). Not only that, but exercise distracts a person from what they are anxious about while it improves attention and working memory. This also helps to turn on executive functioning, which makes problem-solving easier (Ratey, 2019; Lago et al., 2019). Long-term, regular exercise keeps these benefits going, increases executive functioning, and reduces overall anxiety levels for the individual (Ratey, 2019; Audiffren & André, 2019). When supporting a person in creating a regular exercise routine, you should help them find activities that they enjoy. If someone hates to run, they are not going to do it, even when presented with evidence of why it would be good for them. Find an alternative that the person likes, such as walking or dancing instead.

Sensory Activities

For many children, especially autistic children, finding ways to engage with calming sensory activities can be a helpful way to self-regulate. Each person has unique sensory needs, so it is important to discuss sensory preferences and aversions with the child and their caregiver before doing sensory activities. Someone who is auditory seeking, for example, may benefit from listening to or playing music. Someone who is auditory-aversive, however, may self-regulate more quickly in a very quiet or even silent environment. When engaging in sensory activities, consider all of the child's senses, the five we usually talk about: hearing, sight, touch (both light and deep pressure touches), taste, smell, but also additional senses such as proprioception and vestibular awareness. If this concept is new, find affirming trainings focused on supporting neurodiverse children that are presented by an occupational therapist. If the child is seeing an occupational therapist, schedule a consultation to get more information about the child's specific sensory needs, especially those that will help aid in self-regulation.

Mindfulness Activities

Mindfulness activities like breathing exercises, grounding techniques, and progressive muscle relaxation can be a very helpful tool for self-regulation. This is especially true for children who tend toward the freeze response. When introducing mindfulness to children who tend toward the fight response, be sure to include their whole body, such as yoga breathing exercises that pair breathing and body movement.

Drawing

There are many ways to use drawings to support the goals of practicing, problem-solving, and perfecting the CBT skills introduced in this curriculum. Drawing is an important tool because it is fun, reinforcing, and can help increase processing through the use of visual instruction. Drawing also takes time, which slows down any conversation, giving children who have slower verbal processing time to take in the information. The goal is not to be an amazing artist. Stick figures are sufficient if they communicate the desired information.

I am not a good artist and include some of my own drawings to emphasize how you do not need to be to use this strategy. There have often been times that I have started drawing a situation the child is reluctant to talk about, but when they see my drawings, they will take the drawing from me so that they can add their own details because I am doing it "wrong." In this way, my poor drawing skills helped to motivate them to lead the discussion.

Reviewing a Difficult Incident. Sometimes, talking verbally about a difficult incident from the previous week is too hard for a child. If this is the case, try drawing what you know about the incident, inviting the child to give input. If the child continues to express verbally or demonstrate through behavior that they do not want to discuss an incident, even with drawings, you should respect this. A child should not be forced to discuss something they are not ready to discuss. Changing the method of discussion from verbal language to drawing, however, may make the conversation easier for them to handle. Start the drawing and pay attention to the child. As with any intervention, remember that the goal is maintaining the relationship and respecting the child's autonomy.

Review the Possible Outcomes of Different Choices. Another way to use drawings to practice CBT tools is to discuss a particular incident, what happened, and what might have happened if the child made a different choice. For example, at the beginning of the previous chapter, James shared a time that he got to a 5 and hit his sister. Using drawings, James and his therapist can discuss what might have happened differently if he had chosen to punch his punching bag *instead* of hitting his sister. This is a way to look at how changing behaviors can change outcomes as well as subsequent thoughts and feelings. As with any of these drawing activities, it is important to let the child lead the discussion.

In Figure 7.1, the column on the left outlines what actually happened. The column on the right outlines what could have happened if a different response had been made. The first column includes four rectangles showing from top to bottom what actually happened: 1. my sister took my toy, 2. I got to a 4, 3. I got to a 5 and hit my sister, and 4. I was sent to my room. The second column includes four rectangles showing from top to bottom what might have happened if another choice had been made. From top to bottom: 1. my sister took my toy, 2. I go to a 4, 3. I told Dad and hit my punching bag, 4. I got my toy back and my sister was sent to her room.

What happened...

What could have happened...

1) my sister took my toy.

① my sister took my toy.

2) I got to a 4.

② I got to a 4.

3) I got to a 5 & hit my sister.

③ I told Dad & hit punching bag

"Dad!"

I got my toy.

4) I was sent to my room.

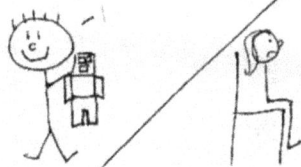

④ My sister was sent to her

Figure 7.1 What happened vs. what could have happened. Drawing by the author.

Discuss the perspectives of self and others. When someone is very upset, it can be difficult to think about another person's point of view. This can be more difficult for children who struggle with understanding neurotypical social rules or understanding nonverbal communication (American Psychiatric Association, 2022). The use of drawings in this case can be helpful in reviewing the child's point of view, as well as the other person's point of view. The goal is to share perspectives and encourage further conversation and resolution of a conflict or misunderstanding.

Cognitive rehearsal. This CBT strategy is very helpful for individuals with anxiety disorders, but can be especially helpful for autistic people. This is due to one of the traits of Autism being an insistence on routines (American Psychiatric Association, 2022). For upcoming events, or other changes in routines that may cause an autistic child anxiety, it can be helpful to use cognitive rehearsal to review what is going to happen, and help them create a script for how to respond to the new situation (American Psychological Association, 2018). This gives the child time to process, ask questions, plan out how they will act, and plan what they will say ahead of the stressful event. Having a plan should help minimize anxiety. This technique can also be used for transitions that consistently cause the child anxiety, such as when the child is dropped off at school. The child should be involved in creating the drawing and what goes in it.

Figure 7.2 presents the cognitive rehearsal chart with drawings in a comic book format outlining the child's schedule for the first day of school.

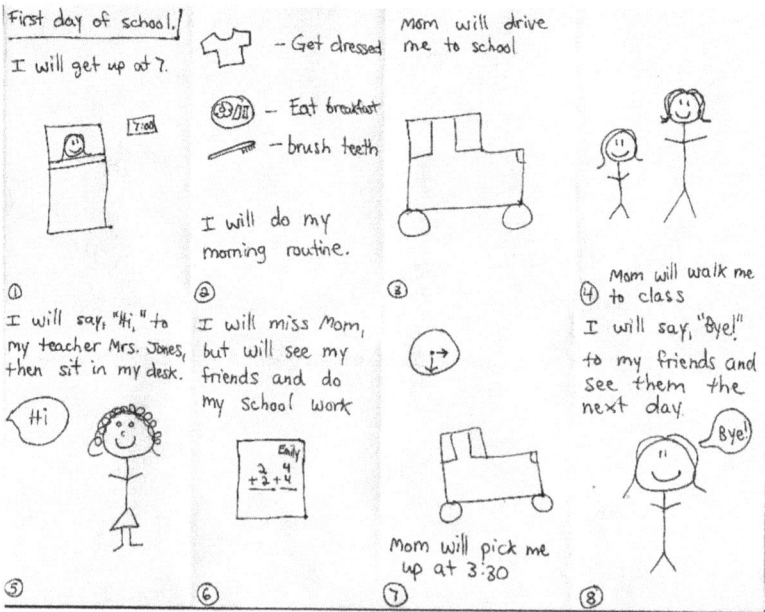

Figure 7.2 Stick figure drawing. Drawing by the author.

Text is arranged in eight total rectangles in two rows. Row one from left to right, rectangle 1 text, "First day of school. I will get up at 7." Rectangle 2, "Get Dressed, eat breakfast, brush teeth. I will do my morning routine." Rectangle 3, "Mom will drive me to school." Rectangle 4, "Mom will walk me to class. Row two from left to right, rectangle 5, "I will say, "Hi," to my teacher Mrs. Jones, then sit in my desk." Rectangle 6, "I will miss Mom, but will see my friends and do my school work." Rectangle 7, "Mom will pick me up at 3:30." Rectangle 8, "I will say, "Bye," to my friends and see them the next day."

Role-Plays

Much of what is outlined earlier can also be done through role-plays, putting on plays using toys or puppets, or using toys and puppets to act out the event. This tool is helpful as the focus is no longer on the child, which can be overwhelming, but on the chosen toy or character. This separation of the event from the individual may make it easier to discuss.

Social Stories

Similar to the use of drawings, Carol Gray's *Social Story* curriculum is a great resource to use with neurodivergent children. A true Social Story must meet ten criteria that are designed to define, give information, support, and create safety for the individual for whom the story was written (Gray, 2024). It is important to follow the format as outlined; otherwise, it is not a true *Social Story*. Also, as with any tool used to reinforce this curriculum, it is important to remember the goals of relationship and child autonomy. It is also important that the Social Story not be used as a tool to show the children that they are doing things "wrong" (Penot, 2024). These stories can, however, be used to explain neurotypical culture for the purpose of taking the mystery out of stressful social interactions. For more information about the use of *Social Stories*, visit Carol Gray's website: https://carolgraysocialstories.com/.

Books

Books and stories are great ways to review, normalize, and start conversations about emotions. Books should be of interest to the child and appropriate for their developmental and chronological age. Here are a few applicable options

- *Alexander and the Terrible, Horrible, No Good, Very Bad Day* by Judith Viorst (1972) (anger)
- *How Do Dinosaurs Say I'm Mad?* by Jane Yolen (2013) (anger)

- *The Little Engine that Could* by Watty Piper (1930) (changing thoughts)
- *Sheila Rae, the Brave* by Kevin Henkes (1987) (anxiety)
- *Today I Feel Silly: And Other Moods That Make My Day* by Jamie Lee Curtis (1998) (emotions)
- *Tough Boris* by Mem Fox (1994) (grief)
- *Wimberly Worried* by Kevin Henkes (2000) (anxiety)

Books: Follow-Up Activities

There are many ways to transition from a book or story to focus on the child. For example, a child can draw themselves and the emotion they are feeling after reading, *Today I Feel Silly: And Other Moods That Make My Day*, or draw a picture of themselves titled, "Emily the Brave" after reading *Sheila Rae, the Brave*. Books can be a conversation starter to discuss hard topics like grief or worry, or can emphasize how thoughts can change behaviors. As with any of these activities, there is room for the creativity of both the child and the therapist.

CBT Triangle

The CBT triangle (Figure 7.3) is a visual tool that demonstrates the ways that an individual's thoughts, behaviors, and feelings interact. This tool is often used to have conversations about how changing one corner of the triangle can help the individual change the other two corners. For example, instead of focusing on a new challenge and telling themselves that they cannot do something, the person might identify a time that they met an even bigger challenge and remind themselves of this when self-doubt creeps in. Once they have identified the alternative thought, the next step is to discuss how this new thought changes, or may change, their feelings and

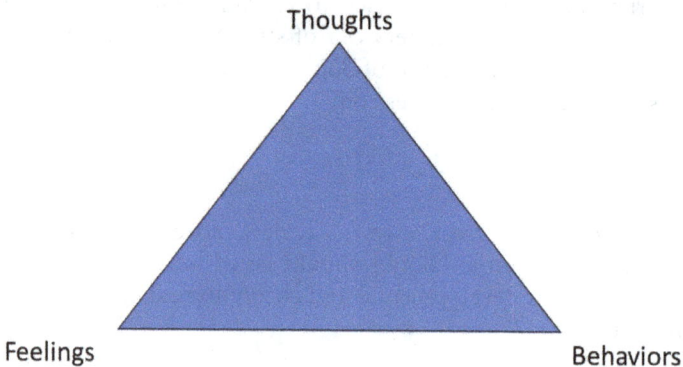

Thoughts

Feelings   Behaviors

Figure 7.3 CBT triangle. Graphic by the author.

behaviors. Not all children or teens who engage in this curriculum will be ready for this CBT tool, so use clinical judgment to assess whether this activity would be appropriate for the individual.

A diagram connecting thoughts, feelings, and behaviors that includes a blue triangle with a word placed in each corner. The word "thoughts" is written at the top, "feelings" on the left, and "behavior" on the right.

Externalizing the Anxiety

Externalizing anxiety is a method of cultivating nonattachment, or to disengage with the anxiety while you wait for it to go away. One way to do this is to remove the anxiety from yourself by giving it a name and personify it, thus making it easier to manage. You do not try to fight against the anxiety, you just work to remove its power (March & Mulle, 1998). Many of my younger clients have called their anxiety something like The Worry Bully. Many teens find it funny to call the anger Karen or Felicia. When the child or teen has an anxious thought, they can then say something like, "That's just my Worry Bully talking. I am going to color while I wait for it to go away." Or for a teen, they can say, "Stop Karen! No one likes you," or simply, "Bye Felicia." With younger clients, you can do activities like drawing the Worry Bully being chased away by their family dog or something similar. Many kids find this strategy to not only be helpful but also a fun way to manage their anxious thoughts.

Incorporating the Child's Special Interest

Make sure that you have identified the child's special interest. This is a great way to build interest, rapport, and make therapy content relatable to the individual. Be creative in finding ways to incorporate a special interest into treatment. For example, a child who loves Disney and is nervous about starting physical therapy may benefit from a review of the plot of the movie *Hercules*, where he had to work with a trainer to get stronger (Clements & Musker, 1997). A child who loves bunnies and is nervous about going to a new place may benefit from seeing pictures of the location with bunnies inserted into the photographs.

Making Additional Tools

Some children may benefit from making multiple emotion scales. For example, they may have started with an anger scale, but would also benefit from making an anxiety scale. They may need a coping list that is specific to school or to soccer practice, as the tools available at home may not be the same as what is available in other activities and locations. They may have enjoyed the anger switches worksheet and want to do worry switches or sad switches as well. Only make additional tools if necessary for treatment and if the child is interested. Otherwise, this activity may become boring and redundant.

The Incredible 5-Point Scale

The Incredible 5-Point Scale: Assisting Students in Understanding Social Interactions and Controlling Their Emotional Responses by Buron and Curtis (2022) is an effective tool not just for use as an emotion scale but also to explain unwritten social rules that may be causing the child anxiety. This book outlines ways you can use this tool to help children gain insight about social situations like bullying, romantic interactions, speaking volume, and many other potentially puzzling social interactions. This tool can also be helpful in facilitating family conversations about such topics. For example, what actions do parents want their child to take when facing a bully or what are family rules about romantic interactions?

Here is an example of how this scale might help define a social interaction that is confusing for a child. One week in the middle of treatment, James comes into session looking sad. The therapist asked her what his highest anxiety level was and he reports that it was a 4. The therapist asked him what got him to a level 4.

"My friend yelled at me and told me to go away," James replied sadly.

"Oh no!" exclaimed the therapist. "I bet you were both anxious and sad."

"Yeah," agreed James. "I don't know what I did. I just hugged him and he got mad."

At this point in the session, his mother explained that James really likes deep pressure, including very strong hugs. His teacher had shared that some of his peers were getting upset because James would run up to them unexpectedly and give them hugs, squeezing as hard as he could. He loved to be hugged like this himself and did not understand that not everyone likes this level of deep pressure. His mother explained that sometimes, this was hard for her as well, especially if she was not expecting a hug, because she was not a fan of deep pressure input.

The therapist asked if James would like to make a hug strength scale, using the same scale they did for his anger and anxiety. He was curious about what this would look like, so they decided that level 1 would be a hug with zero pressure, and a level 5 would be a hug with as much pressure as the person could give. The therapist gave him the homework to check with his family and his friends to find out what level of hug they liked.

The next week, James excitedly shared that his dad liked level 4 and level 5 hugs, but wanted to be asked before getting a 5, that his mom liked level 3 hugs best, and his little brother liked level 2 hugs. He also shared what level of hugs his friends liked and that the scale helped him too because sometimes when he asked for a hug, other people did not hug him hard enough. "Now I can ask for a level 5 hug and get the best squeezes! Mom doesn't squeeze as hard as Dad though, so I decided that her level 5 is more like Dad's level 3.5, so if I want a super good level 5, I ask Dad." His mom added that this was working really well at home and a few weeks later, shared that the teacher reported that peers were no longer complaining that he was squeezing them too hard.

Games That Are Fun, but Cause Level-2 Anxiety

Jenga, Pick Up Sticks, Operation, brain teaser puzzles, and other mildly frustrating games can be a good way to help a child engage in practicing their CBT tools in session. The goal is to just slightly elevate anxiety or reach level 2. You should always consider things like the child's frustration tolerance, how they are feeling in that moment, and their sensory needs. If a child gets frustrated very easily, a frustrating game is probably not a good idea. Similarly, if the child comes to session stating that they had a bad day, a frustrating game will likely increase stress levels beyond level 2. A child with auditory aversions is probably going to go above level 2 when playing a loud game like Operation, so this would not be a good activity for that child.

Social Skills Supports

A Humanistic Approach

As outlined earlier in the introduction, rather than using social skills training, therapists are encouraged to use humanistic approaches, which emphasize building an authentic relationship with the child or teen and give-and-take from both parties, rather than on trying to encourage conformity to neurotypical norms. In order to do this well, this work should start in the first session with the therapist presenting their authentic self, while also building unconditional positive regard for the individual (Gernsbacher, 2006; Payne, 2020). In presenting the therapist's true self, humanistic therapy approaches such as being nondirective, following the child's lead, and use of techniques such as the here-and-now, and transference and countertransference will be used to help the child or teen build confidence in their social skills. Read through the following examples of the latter two examples for how this might look in the therapy setting.

Here-and-Now. The here-and-now is a focus on what is happening immediately in the therapy office between the therapist and client. This is a powerful tool, as it allows the therapist to address issues that may be facing the individual out in the real world within the safety of the therapy office. In other words, social difficulties that the child or teen is running into at home, school, or out in the community are likely to come up in therapy. Instead of teaching formulaic social scripts, the here-and-now will allow the therapist to address these social difficulties in real time (Yalom, 2009). In order to effectively use this tool to build social skills, it is very important that there is strong rapport, or unconditional positive regard, between the therapist and the child. In other words, the child or teen must feel safe and appreciated for who they are in order to benefit from this technique.

Consider the following scenario between Emily and her therapist. Both are on the ground and Emily is playing with the therapist's new fidget toy. The therapist knew that Emily would love this new toy and was excited to show it to her. As expected, Emily squealed in delight when the therapist demonstrated how it worked and then asked if she could play with it. The therapist said, "Of course," and handed it over. After about five minutes, the therapist asked for a turn.

"Not yet," Emily responded distractedly. Another two or three minutes went by.

"Can I have a turn now?" asked the therapist gently. This is when the here-and-now interaction will take place. The therapist knows that Emily is often left out of play by her peers because she struggles to share and take turns with preferred toys. This causes Emily a lot of distress as her parents have explained that she does not fully understand this rejection from peers. When Emily ignored the second request, the therapist kindly says the following, "Emily, I am so happy that you love this new toy. I was so excited to share it with you. Did you know that I also really like this toy and I feel sad and left out right now because I am not getting a turn." The therapist leaves it at this and does not lecture Emily about her difficulties with sharing, or tell her that this is why other children do not want to play with her.

Emily processes this information for a minute or two, and then reluctantly hands the toy over. The therapist gives her a big smile, says "thank you," plays for a few minutes, and then gives the toy back to Emily. The next time that the therapist asks for a turn, Emily sighs, but hands it over without hesitation.

Transference and Countertransference. Similar to the here-and-now is the use of transference and counter transference to help individuals explore their social interactions and build additional skills. With transference, you might explore a child's reactions and expressed emotions that you invoke in them and with countertransference, you explore your own reactions and emotions you have toward your clients. When completing my master's degree, I developed the idea that transference and countertransference was a bad thing and should be avoided. This, however, is not the case. Transference and countertransference are the results of our humanity and the work that goes into building and maintaining a therapeutic relationship. These emotions are data that can be used to help the children and teens whom we are supporting in meeting their social goals (Yalom, 2009).

The following is such an interaction that the therapist had with James. As the two were chatting about a shared special interest, James suddenly blurted out, "What is that you're wearing? It's really weird," referring the therapist's dress, which had a unique pattern with bicycles on it.

"It's not weird, it's unique and fun," responded the therapist, feeling hurt.

"No. It's super weird," replied James, proceeding to name all the reasons that he felt the dress was weird.

The therapist recognized that she was feeling hurt and experiencing countertransference. She also recognized that before responding, she needed to self-regulate in order to ensure that this opportunity to build social skills was therapeutic. She asked James if they could stop talking about her clothing and play a game. He readily agreed. Toward the end of the session, when the therapist was feeling regulated, she asked James if they could talk about his comments about her dress. He looked a little anxious, but said that this would be okay.

"James, when you said my dress was weird and then said a lot of other mean things about it, it really hurt my feelings."

"I'm sorry!" James interjected, his anxiety clearly much higher. "What are you going to do?"

"I'm not going to do anything," stated the therapist, I just wanted to let you know, and to tell you that if you say mean things about what people wear, it will probably upset them and hurt their feelings. You don't have to like everyone's clothes, but it is best to keep those thoughts to yourself." The therapist, then, in an effort to alleviate James's anxiety, stated that they had time for one more game if he wanted to play. James, looking relieved, agreed that this would be a good idea.

Education on Neurotypical Social Rules

Keeping the above scenario in mind, taking time to educate neurodivergent people on neurotypical social rules is a very important part of helping to build social skills. In the scenario, James was not intending to hurt the therapist's feelings, he just did not understand the unwritten social rule that you should not give unsolicited, negative feedback about what someone is wearing. By taking time to explain this rule to James, it helped him to understand that the rule so that he could follow it later.

This is an important step because missing social cues is common for neurodivergent children and adults, especially for those who are autistic. Neurotypical people will often get angry, not understanding that the social misstep was not intended to be rude, but due to not understanding an unwritten social rule. Taking time to review and explain the social rule will help increase the person's understanding of social interactions, therefore decreasing future misunderstandings, and likely decreasing social anxiety for the individual.

When explaining an unwritten social rule, it is important to acknowledge that many social norms and rules do not make sense. For example, in American culture, it is considered rude to ask a woman how old she is. Most people understand this, so avoid that type of question. If you think about this unwritten social rule, however, it is kind of silly. Why should a woman be embarrassed about a fact about herself? Her age is just how long she has been on the planet, why would disclosing that fact be something to be embarrassed by? So, when working to explain a social rule, acknowledge the part that may be illogical, but clear about what might happen if someone were to violate this rule, that is, yes, a woman should not be embarrassed about her age, but if you ask her how old she is, she will likely become angry with you.

The Double Empathy Problem

Another aspect of this issue is the double empathy problem, a concept first outlined by Dr. Damian Milton. What this concept means is that neurotypical people and neurodivergent people often misunderstand one another due to their differing neurotypes. These differences can lead to different ways of understanding, communicating, priorities, and even values (Hartman et al., 2023). Neither one is better than the other, they are just different. Unfortunately, the majority neurotypical culture has often held the belief that neurotypical ways of thinking are preferred, which is why so many Autism interventions focus on teaching autistic people to act more neurotypical. If we want to be affirming and value neurodivergence as an important aspect of human diversity, however, we need to advocate for change, starting with these types of situations with our clients.

If our clients come to us with an issue that is due to the double empathy problem, it is important for therapists to help decode what the different perspectives may be, and then help the person, or the person's support system advocate for their own perspective. For some clients, depending on age and level of support need, they may be able to do this themselves after some coaching in therapy. For others, especially those who are younger or who have more limited ability to communicate, especially in stressful situations, they may need support from others. The end goal should be helping both parties to increase understanding of one another.

Scripting

Traditional social skills training often relies on teaching children conversation scripts. This type of scripting really does not help kids learn genuine back-and-forth communication skills. Scripting can, however, be a beneficial tool to help decrease anxiety for individuals in social situations and is often a tool that neurodivergent individuals, especially those who are autistic, rely on due to tending toward bottom-up processing (Price, 2022). For example, if someone needed to make a phone call that they were nervous about, scripting out what they were going to say before they dialed the number can be a great way to not only decrease anxiety but also help the person avoid struggles remembering what to say or how to say it. For kids, this might be rehearsing a question for their teacher that they are nervous to ask, or practicing how to ask a peer to play a game with them. Writing out a script and role playing in session can be a great way to prepare for a stressful social interaction, and gives opportunity to reinforce the tools, as the therapist can ask for anxiety levels about the interaction before and after the scripting activity, and then after the conversation takes place. "What was your anxiety level when you asked the teacher the question?"

Positive Self-Talk

As kids make progress on managing their anxiety and using their coping skills, encourage them to engage in positive self-talk. For example, when a child shares that they got to a 4, but then remembered to punch a punching bag and not their sister, give praise and then ask them what they can say the next time they go up their anger scale. Statements like, "If I did it when my sister took my toy and I got to a 4, I can do it again." Similarly, if they do something that makes them really anxious, like asking a peer to play a game, they can tell themselves, "I asked a friend to play and they did, so I can ask again."

For some kids, positive self-talk can be a big challenge, as they are used to telling themselves negative things. In this case, practice positive self-talk in sessions. This is something that the therapist and parent can participate in. For example, everyone can say one nice thing about the child, or one nice thing about others in the room. To incorporate modeling, everyone can say three things they like about themselves. This type of activity will help make new habits, and will also normalize saying nice things, rather than negative things, to oneself.

Modifications for Teens

When using this curriculum for teens, you should ensure that the activities are respectful of their chronological and developmental age. Some of the above activities will be appropriate, some will not, and some will need to be adjusted to make them more age-appropriate. For example, you could find more difficult or complicated games and puzzles to play or let the teen take over the drawing, especially if they enjoy drawing. Some teens may also be able to engage more in depth in CBT activities such as reviewing patterns of limited thinking or doing cognitive restructuring worksheets. Again, use clinical judgment and be careful to listen to words and behavior that may indicate that the activity is too difficult.

Can I Add My Own Intervention?

The answer is yes! If you have an activity that you feel will help reinforce the tools in this curriculum, feel free to use it. Just make sure that it follows the guiding principles of the curriculum.

References

American Psychiatric Association. (2022). *Diagnostic and statistical manual of mental disorders* (5th ed., text rev.). American Psychiatric Association Publishing.

American Psychological Association. (2018). *Cognitive rehearsal.* APA Dictionary of Psychology. https://dictionary.apa.org/cognitive-rehearsal

Audiffren, M., & André, N. (2019). The exercise–cognition relationship: A virtuous circle. *Journal of Sport and Health Science, 8*(4), 339–347. https://doi.org/10.1016/j.jshs.2019.03.001.

Buron, K. D., & Curtis, M. (2022). *The incredible 5-point scale: Assisting students in understanding social interactions and controlling their emotional responses* (2nd ed.). 5 Point Scale Publishing.

Clements, R., & Musker, J. (Directors). (1997). *Hercules.* [Film.] Buena Vista Pictures.

Gernsbacher, M. A. (2006). Toward a behavior of reciprocity. *Journal of Developmental Processes, 1*(1), 139–152. https://www.ncbi.nlm.nih.gov/pmc/articles/PMC4296736/

Gray, C. (2024). *What is a social story?* Carol Gray Social Stories. https://carolgraysocialstories.com/social-stories/what-is-it/

Hartman, D., O'Donnell-Killen, T., Doyle, J. K., Kavanagh, M., Day, A., & Azevedo, J. (2023). *The adult autism assessment handbook.* Jessica Kingsly Publishers.

Lago, T. R., Hsiung, A., Leitner, B. P., Duckworth, C. J., Balderston, N. L., Chen, K. Y., Grillon, C., & Ernst, M. (2019). Exercise modulates the interaction between cognition and anxiety in humans. *Cognition & Emotion, 33*(4), 863–870. https://doi.org/10.1080/02699931.2018.1500445

March, J. S., & Mulle, K. (1998). *OCD in children and adolescents: A cognitive-behavioral treatment manual.* The Guilford Press.

Payne, M. (2020). *Modern social work theory* (5th ed.). Oxford University Press.

Penot, J. (2024). *The unmasking workbook for autistic adults: Neurodiversity-affirming skills to help you live authentically, avoid burnout, and thrive.* New Harbinger Publications, Inc.

Price, D. (2022). *Unmasking autism: Discovering the new faces of neurodiversity.* Harmony Books.

Ratey, J. J. (2019). *Can exercise help treat anxiety?* Harvard Health Publishing. https://www.health.harvard.edu/blog/can-exercise-help-treat-anxiety-2019102418096

Schoenfeld, T. J., Rada, P., Pieruzzini, P. R., Hsueh, B., & Gould, E. (2013). Physical exercise prevents stress-induced activation of granule neurons and enhances local inhibitory mechanisms in the dentate gyrus. *Journal of Neuroscience, 33*(18), 7770–7777. https://doi.org/10.1523/JNEUROSCI.5352-12.2013

Sirotiak, Z., Gallagher, B. T., Smith-Hernandez, C. A., Showman, L. J., Hillard, C. J., & Brellenthin, A. G. (2023). Endocannabinoid and psychological responses to acute resistance exercise in trained and untrained adults. *PLoS ONE, 18*(12), 1–12. https://doi.org/10.1371/journal.pone.0291845

Yalom, I. (2009). *The gift of therapy: An open letter to a new generation of therapists and their patients.* HarperCollins.

Caregiver Session

Session 10

Session Objectives

- Check in with parents to interpret:
  - How they feel the child is applying tools
  - Ways to continue to increase application and generalization of tools in the child's natural environment
- Answer parents' questions

Caregiver Session

Now that the child has reached week 10, it is time to check in with the parents or caregivers. The therapist will again be gathering information, answering questions, and problem-solving areas of continued need. The child should not be present so that the parents can speak openly. Ask parents what is going well and what is not going well, and answer any additional questions that they may have about treatment.

This is also the point where clinician will discuss moving toward graduation from therapy by first transitioning to every-other-week sessions. Parents may be anxious about this, so ensure that you listen to concern and share therapeutic reasons for this. Moving to every-other-week session gives the child or teen longer times between sessions to practice the tools independently and also gives them time to process the change that will come with the end of therapy as a support.

DOI: 10.4324/9781003617181-8

Co-parents and Multiple Caregivers

As before, it is recommended to have all parents and caregivers meet together to ensure that everyone receives the same information. If this is not possible, separate sessions can be scheduled. Keep notes of what information you give at each session and ensure that each caregiver receives similar information.

Modification for Teens

This session is optional for teens. Use clinical judgment to determine if a parent session is appropriate.

Practice, Problem-Solve, and Perfecting Skills, Part 2

Sessions 11–13

At this point in treatment, James and his parents all report that he is doing very well. He has stated the last few sessions that his highest anger level has been a 3 and he is able to consistently name coping skills he uses to self-regulate that can be used in a variety of situations. His preferred coping skills are his punching bag and playing basketball. When those are not available, he will snuggle with his blanket or the dog, although his dad reports that this takes him a little longer to regulate. James jokes that he tried to snuggle the cat, but the cat would not cooperate. He also shared a time the previous week when he could not go right to the gym in his school to play basketball right away. He said it was hard, but had been able to trust his teacher when she said that he could go when the clock said 10:45, which was in five minutes. In the past, he would have called his teacher a liar or run out of the room. Now he knows that everyone is working together and listening to his words, so he feels like he can trust them. This made it so he was able wait. His parents agree that he is doing very well. The therapist says that it is time to move to every-other-week sessions. They will see how James does, and then think about graduation from therapy. James looks both proud and nervous, but agrees that he is ready to try this. The therapist reviews with James how he can track how he is doing and when to ask to come in for another session before the two weeks are up if he finds that he is struggling too much.

Session Objectives

- Continue to build and maintain rapport
- Practice, problem-solve, and perfect skills learned
- Work toward independence in use of skills
- Plan for the eventual termination of treatment

DOI: 10.4324/9781003617181-9

Practice, Problem-solve, and Perfect Skills

As with sessions 6–9, these sessions should focus on strategies and activities to reinforce CBT tools. By this point in therapy, you should have a good sense of which children want a variety of activities and which children prefer to do the same activity each session. Listen to the child and follow their lead. The goal is to work toward the independent use of tools. If the child wants a new activity each session, then you need to be ready to change things up. If the child wants to put on the same emotional regulation play with puppets each week and this is helping them to generalize skills at home and school, then, each session should include this type of play.

Each session should continue to include check-ins asking questions such as:

- What was your highest anger/anxiety level?
- How many times did you get to that level?
- What made you get to that level?
- What happened after you got to a 5 (or highest number)?
- What could you do next time instead of (insert unhealthy response here)?

Getting this information at the beginning of session will help inform what activity may be most helpful to practice and reinforce the CBT skills. For ideas of potential activities for these sessions, review content from sessions 6 to 9.

Transition

Transitions are difficult for anxious, as well as autistic individuals, so you need to be mindful of this. For the final third of treatment sessions, it is appropriate to begin this transition. This can be done as simply as mentioning that sessions are coming to an end. Tools such as *Social Stories* and drawings are also useful. The idea is to give the child plenty of time to process and get ready for this transition.

Transition to Every-Other-Week Sessions

Many children will be ready at this point to move to every-other-week sessions. This allows them to have longer stretches of independent practice and to work toward the eventual end of treatment. If they continue to do well during these longer stretches between sessions, this is a good indication that they are on track to graduate. If they begin to struggle more with self-regulation, it is recommended that they return to weekly sessions for at least another four sessions before going back to every-other-week appointments.

Practice, Problem-Solve, Perfect Skills, and Plan a Graduation Celebration

Session 14

Emily and her mother report that she has continued to do well after three every-other-week sessions. The therapist praises Emily for her hard work. After working for the last three sessions on introducing and processing the idea of terminating treatment, the therapist announces that after a parent session, the therapist and Emily will meet one more time for a graduation celebration. "What activities do you want to do for our last session in two weeks?" the therapist asks. Emily responds by naming her favorite therapy games. The therapist writes them down and asks Emily's mother for permission to have a special treat the last session. Her mother agrees and Emily and the therapist plan the celebration.

Session Objectives

- Continue to build and maintain rapport
- Practice, problem-solve, and perfect skills learned
- Work toward independence in use of skills
- Plan for the eventual termination of treatment
- Plan a graduation celebration

Practice, Problem-Solve, Perfect Skills, and Plan a Graduation Celebration

This session should be spent similarly to sessions 11–13, but you should set aside time at the beginning of session to plan the final, graduation session. This step is important, as it not only celebrates progress but also gives the child time to process and get ready for the transition from treatment. This final session, like those previous, should be tailored to the child. This author typically makes a list of favorite activities that the child wants to do with the therapist for the last session, and then plans a special treat to

DOI: 10.4324/9781003617181-10

share together. This may not be appropriate if the child has food allergies or sensitivities, or the caregiver does not approve. However, sharing food is a social action, a way to build togetherness and celebrate with others (Liberman et al., 2016). If for any reason the therapist or family does not feel that sharing a food item the last session is appropriate, the therapist can use a small item like stickers, or inexpensive sensory toy to celebrate the end of mental health treatment.

Reference

Liberman, Z., Woodward, A. L., Sullivan, K. R., & Kinzler, K. D. (2016). Early emerging system for reasoning about the social nature of food. *Proceedings of the National Academy of Sciences of the United States of America*, 113(34), 9480–9485. https://www.jstor.org/stable/26471483

Session 15

Caregiver Session

Session Objectives

• Check in with parents to discuss graduation from treatment

Caregiver Session

At session 15, the child is getting ready to graduate from treatment. It is recommended to schedule this session during the two weeks between sessions 14 and 16 so that there is no longer gap for the child. Both the child and their caregivers may be anxious about this transition. The focus of this session is to give caregiver space to process the transition and discuss any concerns or worries that they have about the termination of treatment. Parent may need encouragement, as well as prompting to use positive self-talk related to their abilities to support their child. It is also appropriate to make a list of signs or symptoms that indicate that the child needs to return to treatment. You should review this list with the parent prior to the next session with the idea that the child will also review and expand upon it.

Co-parents and Multiple Caregivers

If possible, it is recommended to have all parents and caregivers meet at the same time to ensure that everyone gets the same information. If this is not possible due to differing schedules or co-parents who struggle to get along, separate sessions should be scheduled. Keep careful notes of what information you give each session to ensure that each caregiver receives the same basic information.

Modification for Teens

This session is optional for teens. Use clinical judgment to determine if a caregiver session is appropriate.

DOI: 10.4324/9781003617181-11

Session 16

Graduation

Session 16

James and his dad come into session together. James begins his check-in without prompting. He knows the routine well. He reports that his highest anger level was a 3 this week and that he could tell it was going to go higher, so he told his parents what was going on, then went right to the room where his punching bag was and was able to calm down in just a couple of minutes. His dad stated how proud he had been because his sister had taken James's toy after she had been told not to at least five times that day. Before therapy, James would likely have hit her, but he not only did not hit her, but self-advocated by asking his parents for help right away and then going right to his coping skill. His dad shared how James has more trust in them because they are doing a better job at listening to him and he is better able to tell them what he needs.

"That is great James! You should pat yourself on the back." The therapist reached her arm up and modeled what she meant by patting herself on the back. James laughed and did the same. "Are you ready for graduation?"

James replies, "Well, I am happy and sad at the same time."

"That makes sense," states the therapist. "I am happy and sad at the same time too. I am excited for you because you met your therapy goal, but I am sad that I won't get to see you every week."

"What if I start getting mad and hitting again?" James asked with a concerned expression.

"Well, that is one of the things we are going to talk about today, James," the therapist answered. "Last week, your mom and dad and I met to talk about what things to look for that might mean that you need to come back to therapy. We are going to go over that so that you can make sure we got everything right. If you start to get mad and hit again, you just give me a call, and we will see if it is time for you to come back for a few more sessions. After that, we will play and make you a special certificate."

"Okay!" agrees James enthusiastically.

DOI: 10.4324/9781003617181-12

Session Objectives

- A healthy and supportive transition from treatment

Graduation

The focus of this session is to provide a healthy and supportive transition from therapy. This should be celebratory, while also respecting any anxiety that the child may have about losing the support of therapy. Remind the child of the progress that they have made, the tools they learned, and how well they have been using them. Review the list of signs and symptoms that may indicate that the child needs to return to therapy and ask them to add their own items to the list. Then, print out the list or share it on a telehealth platform for future reference.

The remainder of the session should be spent completing the plan made in session 14 such as engaging in the chosen activities, sharing the treat, and finally making a graduation certificate. A certificate can easily be made in a word processing document. Change the layout orientation to "land-scape," and have the child help choose a celebratory font. Add the child's name, what the certificate is for, a line for the therapist to sign and date, and add a picture of the child's choosing and print it out on high-quality paper. For telehealth, upload the certificate into the therapy portal, send via secure email, or mail it to the client.

In Figure 12.1, the text is centered, in blue, using a decorative font: "James Smith has met his treatment goals and is ready to graduate from therapy!" There is a dinosaur representing the happy emotion centered

JAMES SMITH HAS MET HIS TREATMENT GOALS
AND IS READY TO GRADUATE FROM THERAPY!

10/25/25

Dr. Jennifer Cork, DSW, LCSW

Date

Figure 12.1 Graduation certificate. Graphic created by the author.

below. Below the dinosaur is multicolored text written above a solid line that includes from left to right the therapist's signature, and the date the certificate was granted. Under the signature line, written in blue is the therapist's name printed below the signature and the word "date," printed below the date.

Reference

Cup of Couple. (n.d.a). *Dinosaur toys on orange surface.* Pexels. https://www.pexels.com/photo/dinosaur-toys-on-orange-surface-8014524/

Appendix A

Templates

The chart includes six rows and includes eight emotions that are color coded, with spaces to add characters and spaces to include triggers for each emotion. Listed from top row, left to right are four boxes that contain the word "image" that are spaced to add images. The second row includes four color-coded emotions: happy-green, mad-red, sad-blue, and worried-yellow. The third row contains four rectangles that contain the word "triggers," that are color coded to match the emotion above. The fourth row contains four boxes that contain the word "image" that are spaced to add images. The fifth row contains four color-coded emotions: frustrated-orange, excited-light green, bored-gray, and embarrassed-pink. The sixth row contains four rectangles that contain the word "triggers," that are color coded to match the emotion above.

The template includes five rows, representing five levels of anger. Each row is color coded and includes four spaces. The first for the number, the second to add a picture to represent the level, the third to add specific triggers for each level, and the last to add symptoms of each level. The levels of anger are listed from the bottom up: level 1 – green, level 2 – blue, level 3 – yellow, level 4 – orange, and level 5 – red.

The template includes five rows, representing five levels of anger. Each row is color coded and includes three spaces. The first for the number, the second to add specific triggers for each level, and the last to add symptoms of each level. The levels of anger are listed from the bottom up: level 1 – green, level 2 – blue, level 3 – yellow, level 4 – orange, and level 5 – red.

Template created by the author. There are two red circles representing two levels of anger in progressive sizes from small (left) to large (right). Text at the top: How big is my anger? Below this is one small red circle with the word "irritated" written underneath and a large red circle with the words "out of control" underneath.

Template was created by the author. There are three red circles representing three levels of anger in progressive sizes from small (left), medium

Image	Image	Image	Image
Happy	**Mad**	**Sad**	**Worried**
Triggers	Triggers	Triggers	Triggers
Frustrated	**Excited**	**Bored**	**Embarrassed**
Image	Image	Image	Image
Triggers	Triggers	Triggers	Triggers

Figure 13.1 Emotion chart template. Template created by the author.

(middle) to large (right). Text at the top: How big is my anger? Below this is one small red circle with the word "irritated" written underneath, a medium red circle with the word "mad" written underneath, and a large red circle with the words "out of control" written underneath.

There are three yellow circles representing three levels of anxiety in progressive sizes from small (left), medium (middle) to large (right). Text at the top: How big is my worry? Below this is one small yellow circle with the word "nervous" written underneath, a medium yellow circle with the word "worried" written underneath, and a large yellow circle with the word "panic" written underneath.

Template was created by the author. There are three blue circles representing three levels of sad in progressive sizes from small (left), medium (middle) to large (right). Text at the top: How big is my sad? Below this is one small blue circle, a medium blue circle, and a large blue circle.

The text is arranged in two columns with red on the left representing things that turn anger "on," and green on the right representing things that turn anger "off." Text starting at the top: Everyone has things that switch their emotions on and off. Second line: What are things that switch your anger on, and what could you do to switch your anger off? Two rectangles

Rating		What triggers my anger?	What my anger looks like.
5			
4			
3			
2			
1			

Figure 13.2 5-Point anger scale template. Template created by the author.

are placed below the text, red on the left with the word, "on" above it, green on the right with the word "off" above it. The next line of text: On the left, write down things that switch your anger on. On the right, write down things that could switch your anger off. Below the text are five red rectangles on the left with a space to the left to add trigger and five green rectangles on the right with a space to the left to add a coping skill.

Rating	What triggers the anger	What my anger looks like
5		
4		
3		
2		
1		

Figure 13.3 5-Point anger scale template for teens.

The text is arranged in two columns with yellow on the left representing things that turn worry "on," and green on the right representing things that turn worry "off." Text starting at the top: Everyone has things that switch their emotions on and off. Second line: What are things that switch your worry on, and what could you do to switch your worry off? Two rectangles are placed below the text, yellow on the left with the word, "on" above it

How big is My anger?

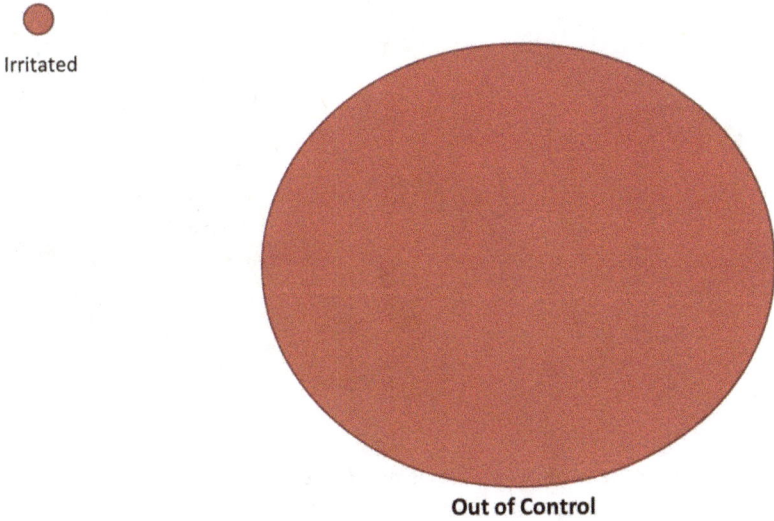

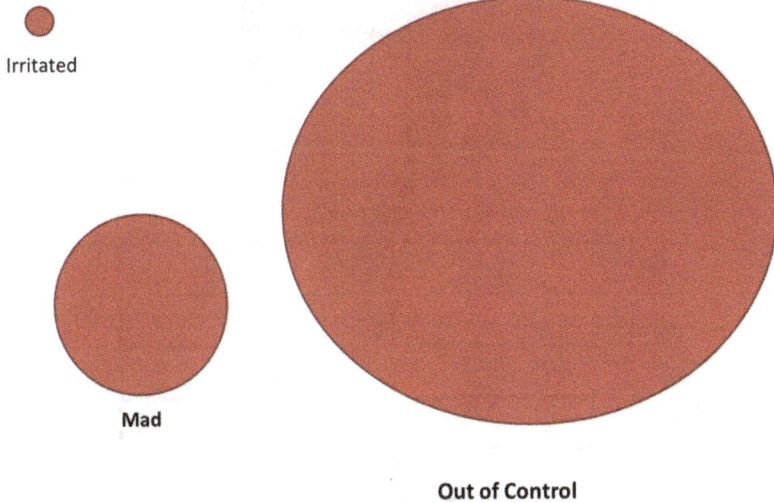

Irritated

Out of Control

Figure 13.4 How big is my anger? Template-2 levels.

How big is My anger?

Irritated

Mad

Out of Control

Figure 13.5 How big is my anger? Template-3 levels.

How big is my worry?

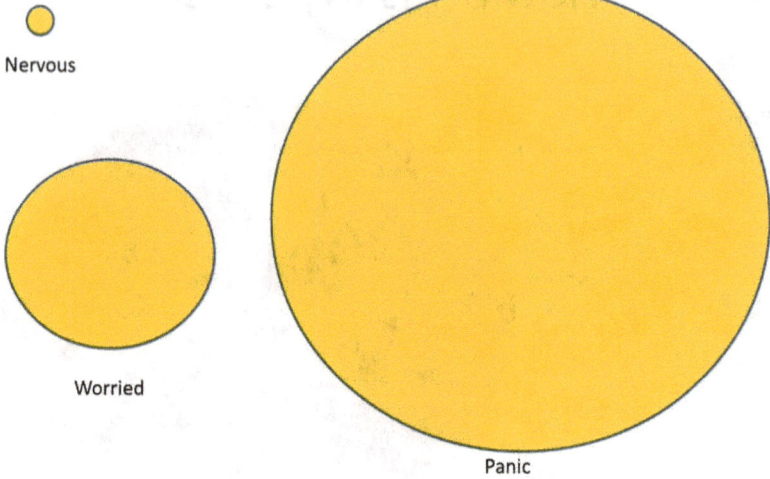

Nervous

Worried

Panic

Figure 13.6 How big is my worry? Template-3 levels.

Everyone has things that switch their emotions on and off.

What are things that switch your anger on, and what could you do to switch your anger off?

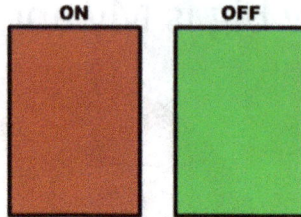

ON   **OFF**

On the left, write down things that switch your anger on. On the right, write down things that could switch your anger off.

Figure 13.7 Anger switches template. Template created by the author.

Everyone has things that switch their emotions on and off.

What are things that switch your worry on, and what could
you do to switch your worry off?

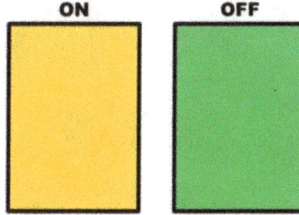

ON	OFF

On the left, write down things that switch your worry on. On
the right, write down things that could switch your worry off.

Figure 13.8 Worry switches template. Template created by the author.

and green on the right with the word "off" above it. The next line of text:
On the left, write down things that switch your worry on. On the right,
write down things that could switch your anger off. Below the text are five
yellow rectangles on the left with a space to the left to add trigger and five
green rectangles on the right with a space to the left to add a coping skill.

The text is arranged in two columns with blue on the left representing
things that turn sad "on," and green on the right representing things that
turn sad "off." Text starting at the top: Everyone has things that switch
their emotions on and off. Second line: What are things that switch your
sad on, and what could you do to switch your sad off? Two rectangles are
placed below text, yellow on the left with the word, "on" above it, green
on the right with the word "off" above it. The next line of text: On the left,
write down things that switch your sad on. On the right, write down things
that could switch your sad off. Below the text are five blue rectangles on the
left with a space to the left to add trigger and five green rectangles on the
right with a space to the left to add a coping skill.

Everyone has things that switch their emotions on and off.

What are things that switch your sad on, and what could you do to switch your sad off?

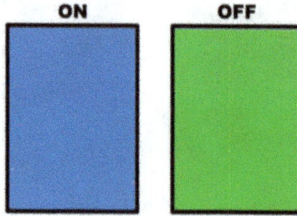

On the left, write down things that switch your sad on. On the right, write down things that could switch your sad off.

Figure 13.9 Sad Switches template. Template created by the author.

FIRST LAST NAME HAS MET THEIR TREATMENT GOALS AND IS READY TO GRADUATE FROM THERAPY!

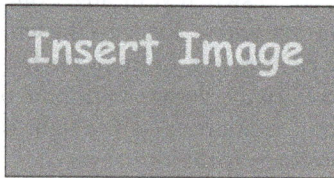

Therapist Name   Date

Figure 13.10 Graduation certificate template. Template created by the author.

Text at the top, "First last name has met their therapy goals and is ready to graduate from therapy!" Text that is to be modified is written in gray, "First last name" to indicate where the individual's first and last name should be placed and "their" to indicate where their pronouns should be placed. The rest is written in blue. Below the text is a gray rectangle meant as a placeholder for an image with the text, "insert image." Below the rectangle is a signature line. Below the signature line is the text: "Therapist Name," and "date."

Appendix B

Recommended Readings

Barkley, R. A. (2020). *Taking charge of ADHD: The complete, authoritative guide for parents* (4th ed.). Guilford Press.

Buron, K. D., & Curtis, M. (2022). *The incredible 5-point scale: Assisting students in understanding social interactions and controlling their emotional responses* (2nd ed.). 5 Point Scale Publishing.

Greene, R. W. (2010). *The explosive child: A new approach for understanding and parenting easily frustrated, chronically inflexible children.* HarperCollins.

Hallowell, E. M., & Ratey, J. J. (2005). *Delivered from distraction: Getting the most out of life with attention deficit disorder.* Ballantine Books.

Hallowell, E. M., & Ratey, J. J. (2011). *Driven to distraction (revised recognizing and coping with attention deficit disorder.* Simon & Schuster.

Price, D. (2022). *Unmasking autism: Discovering the new faces of neurodiversity.* Harmony Books.

Siegel, D. J., & Payne Bryson, T. (2011). *The whole-brain child: 12 revolutionary strategies to nurture your child's developing mind.* Bantam Books.

Silberman, S. (2015). *Neurotribes: The legacy of autism and the future of neurodiversity.* Penguin Random House.

Wise, S. J. (2022). *The neurodivergent friendly workbook of DBT skills.* Independently Published.

Yalom, I. (2009). *The gift of therapy: An open letter to a new generation of therapists and their patients.* HarperCollins.

Index

Note: Numbers in *italics* indicate a figure.

For Product Safety Concerns and Information please contact our EU
representative GPSR@taylorandfrancis.com
Taylor & Francis Verlag GmbH, Kaufingerstraße 24, 80331 München, Germany

*9 7 8 1 0 4 1 0 1 9 7 5 6 *